The Psychology of Religion for Ministry

 *Integration Books*

STUDIES IN PASTORAL PSYCHOLOGY, THEOLOGY, AND SPIRITUALITY
Robert J. Wicks, General Editor

The Psychology of Religion for Ministry

H. Newton Malony

Integration Books

paulist press/new york/mahwah

Acknowledgments
The publisher gratefully acknowledges use of the following: the King and
Hunt Scales (Measures of Religiosity), used by permission of Morton King,
Ph.D. and Richard A. Hunt, Ph.D.; the Age Universal I (Intrinsic)—E (Extrin-
sic) Scale, used by permission of Richard L. Gorsuch, Ph.D.; and the *Religious
Status Inventory*, used by permission of David E. Massey, Ph.D. and Mark
Faraco-Hadlock, Ph.D.

Copyright © 1995 by H. Newton Malony

Library of Congress Cataloging-in-Publication Data

Malony, H. Newton.
    The psychology of religion for ministry/H. Newton Malony.
        p.   cm.—(Integration books)
    Includes bibliographical references.
    ISBN 0-8091-3483-7
    1. Psychology, Religious.   2. Pastoral psychology.   3. Pastoral
counseling.   I. Title.   II. Series.
    BL53.M365 1995
    253.5′2—dc20   94-41661
                                                                    CIP

Published by Paulist Press
997 Macarthur Boulevard
Mahwah, New Jersey 07430

Printed and bound in the
United States of America

Contents

Contents

Foreword

With the compassion of a person with extensive ministerial experience and the insight of a recognized scholar, H. Newton Malony confronts the question: "What can the psychology of religion tell me that I don't already know?" In the process of doing this he raises other more specific questions which touch at the heart of what it means as religious professionals to reach out to others in need.

Among these thought provoking questions are:

—What does "being religious" mean from various psychological perspectives?
—How does religion meet the myriad needs of different people?
—What is religious maturity?
—Does faith really make a person better?
—What, if any, is the relationship between religious belief and a life of health and happiness?
—What can research teach us about the practical, essential elements of preaching?
—How can persons in ministry be more effective leaders?
—What can professionals in religion contribute to the religious experiences of others?

For too long the psychology of religion field has been accessible only in advanced courses, college texts or scholarly journals. Yet the pastors, chaplains, youth workers, religious educators in parishes, and others in ministry had no ready entry into the world of this useful and stimulating material.

In this book, Dr. Malony summarizes, applies, and inte-

1

grates a wealth of material in this essential area and offers it in a succinct, yet amazingly comprehensive work. I hope this book will find its way into parishes, seminaries, graduate schools of religion, but most of all onto the bookshelves of ministers who "work in the trenches" of religion. After having read his work, I think all of them will leave with a better understanding of the role psychology can play in ministry, *their* ministry. And for offering such a service in the preparation of work that can do this, I think Dr. Malony deserves a great deal of gratitude.

Robert J. Wicks
Series Editor

Preface

Most ministers know very little about the psychology of religion. This may sound like an overstatement. Is it not true that a number of psychologists, Freud, Jung, James, and Fromm, for example, have written books about religion which are well known? Furthermore, is it not also true that many books have been written by psychologists for religious persons? In fact, the shelves of most bookstores are filled with titles on religious psychology of one form or another. Then, how can it be said that "most ministers know very little about the psychology of religion?" A possible explanation follows.

The **psychology** of religion could be defined as the study of the behavior of **religious** persons. There is a vast difference between this and popular religious psychology which is usually directed toward helping persons apply the teachings of their faith in their individual lives. There is also a difference between this and theoretical treatises about why people are religious. **Psychologists of religion**, as I am using those terms, have been much more interested in describing, rather than changing or explaining, religious behavior.

Psychologists have been studying religious behavior for almost a century, but for two major reasons little of what they have discovered has filtered down to the average minister. On the one hand, because some psychologists tended to reduce religion to such motives as the child's need for security, many clergypersons have assumed that *all* psychologists explained religion away as nothing more than the projection of infantile needs. In reaction to such an assumption, ministers might think, "Why study the ideas of those who believe that what you have given your life to is meaningless?"

3

On the other hand, because psychologists have often focused their total attention on religious **experience**, ministers
have assumed that psychologists were only interested in feelings, not beliefs. In reaction to this assumption they might ask,
"Almost everyone agrees that thoughts are as important as
emotions; why listen to the ideas of those who don't think beliefs are important?"

These assumptions that psychologists always reduce religion to childlike motivations, or are only interested in religious
emotions contain only partial truths. While it may be true that
some psychologists have tried to explain religion away, more
often than not they have simply limited themselves to describing how religion seemed to be tied in with the basic needs that
all people have or to demonstrating that religion was similar in
many ways to other intense human experiences. Like William
James, one of the earliest psychologists of religion, most psychologists have stated that they could not answer the question
of whether there was a God or not. Following James' lead, they
have been content to limit their study to the behavior of those
who claimed that they did believe in the divine. They have resisted using psychology to prove or disprove religion.

Thus, since they did not take a stand on whether God existed, or which God was better than another, it is only natural
that most psychologists of religion have tended to deal with the
feelings and actions of religious persons; i.e., with those experiences labeled **religious**. They have, indeed, shied away from
evaluating "beliefs." It would be false, however, to think that
no psychologists have studied religious **beliefs** or that *all* psychologists were themselves **non-believers** who explained religion away or who did not consider what people believed to be
important. Increasingly, psychologists have begun to study
what people believe as well as what they experience **when** they
believe. What religious persons think is becoming just as important to psychologists as how and why people act as they do.
Today's psychologists of religion do not limit themselves to
feelings. Moreover, many of them consider religion to be valuable—both for themselves and for others.

As interesting as it might be to explore clergy suspicions
about the psychology of religion or to explain why ministers

have avoided the subject, it may be even more important to state some reasons **why** ministers **should** concern themselves with the topic. Most have only limited time for reading and if a topic, like the psychology of religion, will not enhance their daily work they will probably not spend their time studying it—even if they no longer think it contains irrelevant ideas! Many Protestant clergy will well remember the attitude with which many of them approached classes in their seminary days. As student pastors of small churches, they felt the bind of time and energy and, in anticipation of sermons they had to deliver, they asked of every lecture, "Will it preach?" This pressure to focus on what information can be used is still fashionable for most parish priests and congregational ministers.

The initial reason why the psychology of religion should be of interest to professional religious leaders is that "religion," as I am using this term, applies to **organized**, **institutional** religion—not to religion in general or private spirituality. Two standard definitions of religion illustrate this preference for defining religion institutionally. One definition portrays religion as the ways in which people meet their needs to understand the tragedies, the mysteries, and the injustices of life. The other definition portrays religion as a group of people gathered together around a transempirical idea. Put these two definitions together and religion could be understood as groups of people who meet their needs to understand life's tragedies, mysteries, and injustices by belief in a transcendent reality. Thus, you have organized religion.

My focus in this book will be the psychology of religion defined in this circumscribed way, namely, the behavior of persons who meet their religious needs through congregational life. Of course, **institutional** religion is not all there is to religion, but it is all I am going to deal with here. The chapters will include the results of psychological research that can be applied to the parish. Congregational life is the way the average person is religious, and that is the type of religion with which I am concerned in this book. This should perk up the interest of those who want to do a better job of leading local churches. These ideas are practical; these ideas "will preach"!

As an example of how the psychology of religion can be

helpful to ministers, consider the idea that no religion, however valid and exalted it may be, will be of any worth unless it touches persons in their individual lives. Belief in a given religion, like every other option presented to people—be it to buy a car, learn to square dance, or study Greek literature—will not be attended to or accepted if it does not meet a human need. Searching the want-ads in the newspaper is a clear example of this process. Only when we have a desire to buy a used car or a dresser or a musical instrument or a baby stroller, to name only a few examples, will we turn to the advertisement section. At other times, we will just ignore that part of the newspaper or throw it away.

Every religion, everywhere, must be filtered through needs and wants if that religion is to be received and applied to human life. Psychology is the study of how religious thoughts, words, feelings, and actions relate to these basic human desires. The **needs** that religion meets are **basic** because every life includes tragedies, mysteries, and injustices. No humans escape these experiences. The "business" of the church is to meet these needs in a manner that is better than any other alternative people might find as they search the want-ads of life.

Many ministers may find the above thoughts truisms. The fact that "humans act to meet their needs" is an obvious one. Yet, it is tempting for ministers to see need-based, idiosyncratic behavior among their church members as a necessary evil to be tolerated rather than an opportunity to be understood and utilized. However, all clergy are in the "influence business" whether they admit it or not. Religions do not sell themselves. No religious truths are self-evident. Like buying a new bed or subscribing to a magazine, the need for religion must be awakened and acknowledged.

Of course, it could be said that since religion is **the way** people deal with tragedy, mystery, and injustice, there is no necessity to use psychology to offer suggestions about how best to meet or awaken these needs. From this point of view, all religion needs to do is sit back and wait for people to come when they feel the urge. However, it should be obvious that a significant percentage of the population seems to handle these crises *ir*religiously. It might be conjectured that these people never see a need for religion—even in the midst of their distress. One might wonder to what extent their failure to perceive the value of religion was due to the psychologically-misinformed way in which religion was presented to them. Moreover, other options for cushioning the blows of life might have been more attractive at the time they experienced their need.

Hopefully, however, ministers conceive of the importance of religion in a broader perspective than simply distress-reduction. While clergy recognize the importance of religion for meeting life crises, are they not also convinced of the value of religion for abundant living in everyday experience as well? **Abundant life** is another basic need that religion can meet. The significance of religious faith for these less obvious events also has to be addressed. Here, too, is where psychology has much to offer.

A desire must be created and a want satisfied or the truths of religion will go unheeded. Even a casual perusal of modern life should convince clergy that many people live their lives without any semblance of religious faith. While, ministers might assume that people have an innate need for God, they may be less conscious that people are often unaware of that need. *Needs* must become *wants* and *wants* must become *interests* before people will pay any attention to religious overtures. There is no question of the truth of one church's ritual which states about the church, "All of every age and station stand in need of the means of grace which it, alone, supplies." Yet, unless this basic human need for God is aroused, brought into consciousness, and then directed toward a given church in a specific locale, the "means of grace" which the church has to offer will go unheeded. Religion will be like a product that is offered for sale but which nobody buys!

As the old maxim states, "Some people live for God, some people live for country, some people live for Yale." But it could safely be added, "Unless people self-consciously seek to meet their desires for handling their life crises or for living abundantly through God, through country or through Yale, no one of them will live for any one of the three." This makes psychology a very pragmatic science—and so it is, without apology. In the great tradition of Galileo, psychology leaves to others the determination of "why" human beings are created the way they are and "why" they act as they do. Psychology busies itself with describing "how" people behave once they find themselves in a given predicament here and now.

Thus, understanding the discoveries made by psychologists of religion will enable pastors to more effectively influence the acceptance and application of faith to personal experience in, and through, congregational life. Becoming more effective in influencing persons through the way they conduct their ministries should become a concern for all ministers.

The ability to identify these needs and consciously direct one's message toward meeting them is a skill that can be learned and practiced. While there may be a reluctance to look upon one's ministry as a pragmatic skill, there is the parallel danger that ignoring this fact may lead to professional mediocrity or failure. It is probably as critical to know how normal religious persons behave as it is to be able to interpret religious scriptures in the language in which they were written!

This book is a summary of a number of the conclusions of psychology about religion over the past twenty years. During that period of time some of us have devoted most of our research and writing to these endeavors. A selection of these studies will be reviewed here and their meaning for the work of parish ministry will be described.

Much of our work has been what might be called, for lack of a better term, "basic psychology of religion." Most of this research was originally undertaken in an effort to understand, not change, religious behavior. Reports of these studies have been presented at psychological conventions or published in professional journals read only by social or behavioral scientists. I think it would be safe to assume that few, if any, ministers would have read more than a few of these studies.

It has to be admitted, therefore, that in spite of the intent in this book to apply these ideas to parish ministry, these investigations were not originally undertaken with that purpose in mind. This does not mean that the results have no meaning; only that this was not our prime concern. Yet, as I said earlier, I have always been a churchman, and assisting clergy has never been far from my mind. I identify with my son, a professor of computer science, who stated his own interest thusly: "I am not so much interested in applied research as I am in research that can be applied." In fact, this book might best be entitled: "An *Applied* Psychology of Religion." I am convinced that these studies can be put into practice, and I trust that each of the chapters devoted to one, or more, of them will prove me right.

As an ordained clergyperson who once was a parish pastor, who remains active in a local church and who currently is involved in the institutional life of a denomination, I think I understand the grandeur and also the misery of organized religion. I believe I have the ability to make these findings come alive for clergy in a way that will increase their self-confidence and enhance their ministries.

Before starting this task, a word of caution to the reader should be given. A reader should not expect an exhaustive discussion of everything that *all* psychologists of religion have ever written over the last two decades. What is included here is more limited in its focus. Although I have not confined myself entirely to my investigation, I have emphasized mine and my students' research. We have dealt with some important issues but there are others we have not considered. Hopefully, ministers will find these chapters interesting enough to read other psychologists of religion whose writings I have listed at the end of chapters.

As a preview of what is to come, the topics to be considered in the forthcoming chapters are described below.

The first chapter will consider what it means to be religious from a psychological point of view. A model for religion proposed by the Swedish psychologist, Helmut Sundén, led to an S(stimulus)–O(organism)–R(response) formula for religious experience. Being religious is thereby reconceived in psychodramatic and operant-behavioral terms. The way in which a given religious tradition guides and forms religious experience is related to the functions of dogma as well as of doubt. Hopefully, clergy will be intrigued by the ways psychologists have conceptualized "being religious," and will be stimulated to apply these ideas in their work. In anticipation of this outcome, it is hoped that they will feel the answer to this chapter's title "What can the 'psychology of religion' tell me that I don't already know?" will be "a great deal; tell me more."

"Different strokes for different folks" could be the title of the second chapter. The study of individual differences has been a major concern for psychology throughout this century. The church is the only organization in our culture that seeks to meet the needs of persons across gender, ethnic, age, and temperament differences within the confines of one program in one building. The research suggests that there are some important variations, as well as crucial similarities, in the way religion meets the needs of different persons. To rely on folk wisdom or biased polemics about these idiosyncrasies is unwise. Unique ways in which religion can be tailored to be most helpfully presented will be noted.

Religious maturity will be the theme of chapter 3. When religion is mature, what does it look like? What do people believe? How do they think? feel? behave? Using the theorizing of the late Menninger Foundation psychologist, Paul W. Pruyser, this chapter will describe efforts to determine and diagnose mature religion. Religion is herein understood within the framework of classical Christian beliefs rather than in terms of psychological processes. "Functional theology" is the term that has been used to describe the manner in which affirmation of the truths of the Christian revelation are practiced in effective daily living. This chapter will describe measures designed to be used by ministers in pastoral counseling and spiritual direction.

"Religion and Morals: Does Faith Make Better Persons?" is the title of the next chapter. Since the 1930s, psychologists have been studying the relationship between ethics and religion. The results have been mixed. Sometimes being religious has been correlated with moral behavior, while at other times it has not. A related question that has been asked is whether certain beliefs or types of religion seem to inspire more ethical behavior than others. One interesting type of study has been the investigation of whether intentionally prompting people to act unselfishly results in actual altruistic behavior or not. Several of these studies are described and related to congregational programs and practices. Changing behavior and inculcating values are probably prime religious goals for most clergy.

Chapter 5 considers a topic about which much has been written in the popular literature—religion and health. The results of controlled research have not been clear. However, recent studies imply that certain types of religion do, in fact, provoke good mental, and even physical, health. Scriptures have always promised joy and contentment. Christian belief has promised abundant life here as well as eternal life hereafter. It should come as no surprise when research confirms that mature faith does correlate highly with adjustment and even with resistance to disease. While religion probably should not be construed as entitling persons to health and happiness, there does seem to be a relationship which cannot be denied.

"Are Sermons Better Than Sleeping Pills?—The Boon and Bane of Preaching," is the title of the next chapter. Here is a topic in which all ministers will, or should be, interested in spite of the fact that preaching is given more importance in some traditions than others. Most homiletics classes have not included reports of the research on sermonic effectiveness. Nor have practice preaching classes considered the reports that almost two-thirds of churchgoers report they go to sleep during homilies and sermons. While it is obvious that preaching is, by no means, all that pastors do, preaching remains a prime basis on which ministerial effectiveness has been judged. Using the research on preaching, practical ways to improve the preparation and presentation of sermons will be considered.

Chapter 7 will continue a discussion of clergy performance. Psychologists have studied religious leaders for some time. They have been very involved in predicting effectiveness and in the evaluation of ministerial candidates. Much is now known about the characteristics of good congregational leadership. A fourfold model for "having effect" is related to studies about roles, communication and styles of leadership. Although there is no need to conclude that all pastors should be alike, there are definite approaches that will enhance support or erode it. If clergy would be effective, intentional leadership, as opposed to that which is impulsive or intuitive, is encouraged.

"Today's 'Damascus Roads'—The When, Where, and

How of Religious Experience," is the title of chapter 8. Over the last three decades the news has been filled with reports of 'conversion,' 'charismatic,' 'born-again,' and 'mystical' religious experiences. When and where do these occur? Is there any consistency and/or predictability to them? Several noteworthy studies have sought to understand these events. The conclusions from research on conversions to new religions, on renewal and charismatic experiences, and on the models that have been utilized to explain these events will be described. Although no ministers should be so bold as to ever conclude that they could completely control religious experience, a better understanding of some of these dynamics can be had.

One word of explanation is needed before turning to the chapters described above. Typical research articles on psychology are almost incomprehensible to non-psychologists. They are filled with statistics, tables, and off-hand references to other research with which it is presumed the reader is well acquainted. Even the graduate students with whom I work often have to take refresher courses on how to read and understand research when it comes time for them to undertake their own investigations. None of this obscurantism will be found here!

There will be few, if any, numbers used to describe results. However, where conclusions are noted, readers will occasionally see the phrase "significant differences." This will mean that what was reported could have happened less than five times in a hundred by chance alone, and that the authors of the studies concluded that something else (for example, environment, past experience, faith) caused what happened to occur. Hopefully, this exclusion of statistics and other jargon will make the chapters readable without insulting the intelligence of ministers who are seeking some new ways to look at their tasks. Nevertheless, at the end of each chapter are a list of references which interested readers may pursue should they desire.

I once read an anecdote about philosophy that I hope will not apply to readers' opinions about psychology after they finish reading this book. It seems that in the men's toilet of a philosophy department of a certain university, the walls were comparatively free of the graffiti that is common in many public facilities. In desperation, someone had written, "Why are these walls so clean?" to which someone had replied, "Because philosophers no longer have anything to say." My goal of helping ministers become more effective would have failed if readers felt that way about this volume.

Readers are encouraged to duplicate the material in the Appendices in order to assist them in their ministry. Full permission is granted for such duplication.

Chapter 1

Being Religious—A Psychological Point of View

There are, indeed, "varieties" of religious experience, as the title of William James' famous book[1] indicates. Yet, they all fit into a Stimulus(S)–Organism(O)–Response(R) formula, from a psychological point of view. Whether we consider

—Moses and the burning bush,
—Abraham preparing to sacrifice Isaac,
—Jacob wrestling with the angel,
—Mary Magdalene meeting the angel at the empty tomb,
—Paul hearing Jesus address him on the Damascus road,
—Martin Luther's nailing his 95 Theses to the church door,
—Ignatius divining his Exercises,
—Wesley's heart-warming experience on Aldersgate Street,
—James' once-born or twice-born Christians,
—Confirmands at their first communion,
—Converts at a Billy Graham crusade,
—Midnight worshipers at a cloistered monastery,
—New recruits to the Salvation Army,
—Charismatics praying in tongues,
—Celebrants at a pontifical mass,
—Church members with open Bibles listening to a teacher, or
—Persons "slain in the spirit" at a healing crusade,

it does not matter. From a psychological point of view they are all the same. In all these cases, and thousands of others that

15

could be added, there is a **stimulus(S)** to which people **respond(R)** after they have reflected on the event (**organism, O**). This is the one, and only, way humans have of being religious.

I call this the "S-O-R Model of Religious Experience."[2] This model probably reminds many of us of our first course in psychology where we studied Ivan Pavlov who conditioned his dogs to salivate when a bell was rung. In many of these psychology courses, this stimulus-response or S-R formula was proposed as the basis for **all** human behavior, be it lovers' tears of joy when they embrace, or the anticipation scholars feel when they begin a lecture, or the awe worshipers experience when the priest elevates the host, or the conviction marchers feel when they protest injustice. All behavior is conditioned, or learned, in a stimulus-response sequence. No behavior occurs spontaneously. Only eating and sleeping are instinctual. Being religious is no different from being law-abiding or being a ballet dancer or being a bank teller—all result from some learned response to some stimulus.

The only thing wrong with Pavlov's model was that it presumed dogs and people were alike; their learning occurred automatically, outside conscious awareness. His formula lacked any intentional awareness or self-conscious thought. The O (organism) in my S-O-R formula was missing. As far as we know, consciousness is a uniquely human capacity; it is not an ability that dogs possess—at least to the degree that we experience it.

Now, I acknowledge that who does and who does not possess consciousness is not a completely settled issue. Pavlov's dogs, like the canine pets that many of us have owned, wagged their tails when he came into the laboratory. They seemed to recognize and respond to him in a way that suggested conscious awareness. Yet, Pavlov's dogs learned new behavior only in connection to eating. They did not seem to rise above basic instinctual needs. Human behavior, especially religious behavior, seems to be on a much higher plane than this. While many of us might feel that religion is as basic a need as the need for food, few of us would conceive religious experience as synonymous with unconscious salivation to the sound of a bell when we were hungry. Religious behavior is more than this.

The Importance of the O in the S-O-R Formula

This is where the "O," or organism, comes in. Being religious fits an S-O-R, not an S-R, formula. Religious behavior is conscious, intentional, and thought-filled! The religious stimulus (S) is taken in, perceived, mulled over, experienced, and thought about before it is responded to. The response does not occur outside consciousness; it is not automatic. The response is a "response," not a "reaction"—the term that is often applied to behavior that is instinctual or conventional.

I recognize that some religious behavior appears conventional and entirely dependent on fashion or custom. It often looks as if it is automatic and habitual. Sometimes it seems as if it is just doing what everyone else is doing. Yet, in most cases we place a value judgment on this type of religion. Churches that affirm "believer baptism" do not consider attendance or participation valid religious behavior until persons have made a religious decision on their own. Even churches that affirm that the baptism of infants is sufficient for salvation include confirmation in their practices, a ritual where children assume for themselves the vows made for them as infants.

William James wrote about the centrality of the "O(organism)" or personal experience in religion. He noted how difficult it is to inspire second-generation religionists who were conditioned to be religious by their parents. He called this hand-me-down or second-hand religion and contended that, without re-experiencing, this type of religion would never be as vital and alive as that of the parents. Personal thought and conscious intention, the "O" in my formula, would seem to be an essential ingredient of being religious.

G. Stanley Hall; An Example of the "O"

G. Stanley Hall, the first president of the American Psychological Association, proposed a theory of conversion that illustrates the importance of personal thought and feeling, the "O" in my S-O-R formula, for religious experience. In his book, *Jesus the Christ in the Light of Psychology*,[3] Hall suggested that the heart of the Christian religion was altruism or unselfish love. He thought that conversion was the process whereby persons were transformed from self-love into love of others. He assumed that people were born with the potential to make this transition but through the years of growing up they became self-centered and selfish. According to Hall, people needed a process to change them back to the potential with which they were born.

In trying to answer the question of how such a transformation could come about, Hall rejected any automatic or instinctual answers. The transformation had to occur in each individual through a thoughtful, self-conscious process. Hall contended that conversion could not be wrought by reason alone, because reason would turn to pragmatism and self-interested functionalism. Reason would only confirm the resistance which was already there. Nor could conversion be wrought by moral example, as in looking to Jesus as a great martyr. Jesus' loyalty to his ideals might inspire some, but Hall contended that most people would simply admire Jesus but not follow him. Only the story of a God who loved others enough to die for them was radical enough to induce conversion in people's hearts.

Hall's theory was that Jesus embodied "man-soul"—the dormant potential deep inside every human being that people could plainly see lived out on the cross. Becoming aware of their potential by looking to Jesus awakened humans' sense of identity with Jesus and, thus, transformed them from self-love to love of others. Faith in Jesus, according to Hall, effected conversion not because of guilt, or rationality, or idealism but because of a spiritual sense of kinship in the center of their beings which was awakened by the crucifixion.

Hall used the image of a "geode" to illustrate this idea. By the time of adolescence, according to Hall, people had encrusted their inner love of others with the rough, uneven cover of selfishness. When their kinship with Jesus was awakened by the story of God's love on the cross, the "geode" of self-centeredness was broken open and the beautiful, inner core of unselfish altruism was revealed. Similarly in geology, when geode stones are cracked open they reveal lovely crystal centers.

I describe Hall's point of view, not because of the necessary truth of its implicit theology, with which one might or might not agree, but because it illustrates the important inclusion of the individual in the S-O-R model. Hall would agree that being religious is something one does intentionally and self-consciously after thoughtful evaluation. It can never be reduced to a Pavlovian S-R formula wherein religion is identified with instinctual salivation at the ringing of a bell.

The Stimulus (S) in the S-O-R Model: God/Need

Having established that what happens inside the person, the "O" in the S-O-R formula, is important, I would like to describe the other components of this psychological model of religious behavior more fully. A table of depicting perspectives on the Stimulus (S), as well as Response (R), follows:

Table 1-1
Perspectives on the Three Dimensions in the S-O-R Model[4]

	Event 1	Event 2	Event 3
Psychological Perspective	Stimulus→	Organism→	Response
Theological Perspective	God→	Faith→	Worship/Work
Alternate Psychological Perspective	Need→	Perception/ Conception→	Action

Examination of this table should show how the three dimensions of the S-O-R model relate to more familiar ways of thinking about what it means to be religious. It is typical to speak about religious persons as those that have faith in God who has revealed himself to them. Further, faith leads to work or response. This is true, not only in the New Testament book of

James but in everyday life where religious persons are expected to act ethically.

The experience of Samuel in the Old Testament illustrates these relationships (1 Samuel 3:1–11). While attending to the lamps in the temple one evening, the boy Samuel heard a voice call his name. After telling Samuel several times that he was not calling him, Eli, the priest, realized it was God's voice that Samuel was hearing. He advised Samuel to respond the next time he heard the voice with the words, "Speak, Lord, your servant hears." God spoke and Samuel listened. On the basis of his conviction that God wanted certain things done, Samuel undertook the task of becoming judge over Israel and of choosing the first king. In this story, God was the stimulus. He revealed himself to Samuel. Samuel listened and had faith, the "O" or organism in the formula. And he responded by undertaking the work God called him to do. Revelation, faith, work—Samuel illustrates a common way of talking about being religious.

However, a less familiar way of thinking about religion is illustrated by the alternate psychological perspective where the stimulus is depicted as a "need." In the Preface, it was asserted that no behavior occurs unless it meets a need. In other words, all behavior is motivated. Certainly that was true of Pavlov's dogs. But in what sense is this true in a religious experience? Was Samuel looking or listening for God? If so, he didn't act like it. He thought Eli was calling him, not God. Eli had to redirect Samuel's attention to God. Where was Samuel's need?

One way this problem has been solved has been to say, "Everybody has a need for God." St. Augustine implied this when he stated, "Thou has made us for Thyself, and our hearts are restless until they find their rest in Thee." However, it might be asked, "Are people's hearts restless for what God has to offer? or for God himself?" Psychologists are inclined to focus more on the former than on the latter; more often they see people seeking what God has to offer than for God himself. They see people who are anxious or insecure or guilty or sad. And then they see people who have faith in God become calm, peaceful, forgiven, happy and confident.

People have needs that faith in God meet. Saying it that

way makes more sense to psychologists. They would agree with the definition of religion as "the way people deal with the mysteries, the enigmas, and the tragedies of life." Mysteries are those imponderables such as worry over the origins of the universe and the meaning of life. Enigmas are those life experiences in which goodness does not always win and fairness does not always succeed. Tragedies are those events where the fabric of life is torn apart by death, by evil, and by accidents. Religion has answers to all of these.

When ministers bless worshipers with words like, "Now may you have the peace that passes all understanding and the understanding that passes all peace," they are intoning the time-honored truths of faith where the Christian God meets persons at their deepest needs to comfort as well as challenge them. He challenges them to deal with life's mysteries in a manner that evokes their commitment to an ethical, altruistic, and just understanding of life's meaning and purpose, and he comforts them in the midst of misfortune and suffering.

Of course, there remains the problem of understanding the type of religious response such as Samuel's in the temple—religious experience which does not seem to occur in reaction to any need. Samuel was just there; he was not looking for God. Or was he? When God spoke to him he was in the temple; he was not at play, at school, or at dinner. Temples are where gods speak to people. At least, one could say, temples are where we **expect** gods to speak to people. Samuel was in a religious setting, doing religious things.

Hannah, his mother, had determined that Samuel would give his life to God. She had sent him to serve the priest, Eli, at an early age. In much the same way, parents down through the years have provided the environment and even sent their children to religious schools in hopes they would become priests, nuns, and ministers. As one Christian educator said of these parents and of Hannah, "We teach them the answers long before they know how to ask the questions, so that, when they **do** ask the questions, they will already know the answers."

Samuel was prepared. He did not hesitate when Eli told him to go back into the temple and to reply, when next he heard the voice, "Speak, Lord, your servant hears." In an implicit manner, Samuel knew that the answer to his need for understanding the purpose of life lay in God. The same thing probably happened to the Samaritan woman who met Jesus at the well (John 4:1ff) and who, although she did not come looking consciously for the kind of water that she received from Jesus, yet rejoiced and returned to her village eager to tell others what Jesus had done for her. A psychological understanding of religious experience assumes that people have a need for what God can give even when they are not aware of it.

The "R" in the S-O-R Model: Worship/Work

As can be seen in the above table, religious experience is best conceived of as three events rather than one. It involves a stimulus, event 1, an internal perception/conception process, event 2, and, finally, a response, event 3. Taken together, these events comprise religious experience. Religious experience is not complete without all three of these events.

The general public knows this full well. It is common to hear religious critics say, "They say they are Christians but they don't act like Christians." It is as if they are judging religious experience as incomplete unless it has an effect on behavior—what people do. William James stated that good religion should be judged on its "fruits," or effects, rather than on its "roots," or origins in special, paranormal experiences.

The experience of the prophet Isaiah is a paradigm for illustrating how religious experience includes a response, as well as a stimulus and an internal process of perception and conception. In the sixth chapter of Isaiah (1–13), he reports that at the time of the death of the king he went to the temple and "saw the Lord sitting on a throne, high and lofty." This was the stimulus—a vision that came in the midst of a troubled, uncertain time. After describing the vision which he saw, he acknowledged that he was thinking seriously about the event; the "O" in religious experience. He said, "Woe is me! I am lost, for I am a man of unclean lips, and I live among a people of unclean lips; yet my eyes have seen the King, the Lord of hosts!" The vision continued by God assuring Isaiah of pardon and forgiveness, followed by Isaiah hearing God asking, "Whom shall I send, and who will go for us?" Then came Isaiah's response, "Here am I, send me." A clearer "R" in the S-O-R formula cannot be found. He worshiped and he went out to work for God. Psychologists consider Isaiah's experience an excellent paradigm of a complete religious experience.

In the last part of this chapter, I will discuss the way that tradition functions from a psychological point of view.

How Tradition Influences Religious Experience

Tradition determines **how** people are religious, not **whether**. As was noted earlier, basic human anxieties arising from mystery, enigma, and tragedy predetermine people's need for what God has to offer. But these anxieties do not determine **how** this need for God will be met; tradition does that.

To ignore the many types of religion in the world and claim that a given faith is the only way to God would be like the proverbial ostrich who puts its head in the sand and denies reality. On the other hand, to ignore the importance of tradition for the individual devotee would be equally unrealistic. Those parents who state that they intend to not influence their children's faith, thus letting them choose for themselves, will probably end up with children who are not religious. The incidence of religious experience outside of any religious tradition is likely to be less than one in a thousand.

Religious traditions shape and determine the way in which God is experienced; they are important, if not essential. It is perfectly appropriate for people to insist that their tradition is the **best** tradition, although that is not the function of psychology. However, psychology can describe the process through which traditions shape the experience of their followers, and that is what the next section will consider.

The Swedish psychologist of religion, Helmut Sundén,[5] has proposed a "psychodramatic" framework for understanding how tradition influences the ways that people experience God. He suggests that a given religious tradition, such as the Christian faith, describes numerous scenes in which God interacts with humans. For example, the resurrected Christ speaks to disciples on the Emmaus road, and Job disputes with God over his travail. These are called "dual-role" situations which, through religious education, become well-known to worshipers within that tradition.

Through a process of assimilation and identification, persons adopt the expectation that they can have the same type of experience. These adopted "dual-role" expectations function as patterns and structure the perceptual content so that persons often report that they have had "Emmaus road experiences" or that they, like Job, "have argued with God" when injustice struck.

These "dual-role" situations become paradigms for how God is experienced by persons within a given tradition. Although they do not limit absolutely the ways in which God is experienced, by any means, they become normative for people and the vast majority of devotees will report their experiences as similar in form to those of one or more of the "dual-role" situations provided them by their religious traditions.

At the beginning of this chapter, I stated that the psychology of religion simply described the behavior of those who believe in God, but took no stand on the truth or falsity of their beliefs. This description of the way in which tradition shapes religious experience is a case in point. Although as a believer myself, I do, indeed, have faith in the ultimate truth of these Christian "dual-role" experiences; as a psychologist I limit myself to agreeing with Sundén that these are the ways any tradition shapes the religious experience of its followers. Sundén's model is a clear illustration of what has been termed the "social construction of reality," whereby the culture in which one lives determines one's perceptual world and provides the framework for day-to-day experience. His model extends this model to religious reality.

Keeping this framework in mind, it can be shown how the model could be experienced within the Christian faith by grouping typical Christian religious experiences under Mystical, Born-Again, Institutional, and Charismatic types, whereby several paradigm "dual-role" relationships can be identified. Pastors will easily recognize these among members of their parishes. They may even want to emphasize one or more of these in their preaching and teaching.

Mystical types of religious experience are events in which persons feel they are in the presence of a transcendent reality to which they are essentially related. The result is inner peace, exhilaration and/or inspiration. Examples are Moses and the burning bush (Exodus 3:1ff), God speaking to Elijah at Mount Horeb (11 Kings 19:11ff), and the Psalmist beholding God's ". . . heavens, the work of your fingers, the moon and the stars which you have established, . . ." (Psalm 8:3ff).

Born-Again types of religious experience are events in which life is transformed, sins are forgiven and salvation is assured. The result is a new sense of life's meaning coupled with a sense of God's daily presence and guidance. Examples are Nicodemus becoming as a little child (John 3:1ff), Paul on the Damascus road (Acts 9:1ff), Philip's conversion of the Ethiopian eunuch on the Gaza road (Acts 8:26ff), and the enlightenment of the Samaritan woman at Jacob's well (John 4:1ff).

Institutional types of religious experience are events which occur in settings of worship or fellowship. Worshipers are awe-struck with mystery, meaning and a sense of God's presence. The result is recommitment to religious identity and faithfulness as well as a feeling of being inspired. Examples are the experience of doubting Thomas (John 11:20ff), Samuel in the temple (1 Samuel 3:1ff), Isaiah after the death of the king (Isaiah 6:1ff), the response of the Jews to Jesus' leading worship in the synagogue at Nazareth (Luke 4:16ff), and the command of Moses to take stones from the Jordan River for an altar of remembrance of the Hebrews' safe crossing so that their children would never forget (Joshua 4:1ff).

Charismatic types of religious experience are events in which persons feel their minds, voices, and bodies taken over by the Holy Spirit. The result is a changed sense of consciousness and a feeling of being guided by God. Examples are the Pentecost experience of the early church (Acts 2:1ff), Jacob wrestling with the angel (Genesis 28:10ff), John's being "in the spirit on the Lord's Day" (Revelation 1:9ff), and the disciples on the Emmaus road whose hearts "burned within them" as they walked with Jesus (Luke 24:13ff).

This is by no means an exhaustive list of "dual-role" events within the Christian tradition with which persons may identify and assimilate into their own religious experiences. There are many more. Nor can all these events be grouped under the fourfold typology described above. They do offer, however, examples of how tradition shapes the way in which God is experienced, and they provide a means by which pastors can understand what it means to be religious within the Christian format. Most persons who talk about being religious will report their experience by saying, "I, like Peter . . . ," or "Like Isaiah I . . . ," or "Like the woman at the well I . . . ," or "I, like David . . . ," or "Like Paul I . . . ," etc., etc. This is what religion means from a Christian point of view. These are the images that bring faith down to life for people.

This chapter has considered religious experience within a Stimulus-Organism-Response model and has explored the way in which psychologists understand what being religious means as shaped by specific traditions. In the next chapter we will discuss some of ways that personal traits, as opposed to religious traditions, shape the manner in which individuals apply faith to their lives. Differences between the sexes, between ethnic groups, between the old and the young, and between persons of various motives will be addressed.

For Further Reading

H. Newton Malony, "G. Stanley Hall's Theory of Conversion," *Psychologists Interested in Religious Issues Newsletter*, Fall (1983), pp.3–5.

H. Newton Malony, "The Concept of Faith in Psychology," in *Handbook of Faith*, ed. James M. Lee (Birmingham, AL: Religious Education Press, 1990), pp. 71–95.

Chapter 2

Boys and Girls, Black and White, Young and Old: Do People Differ in the Way They Are Religious?

In the last chapter, I noted that people had a variety of religious experiences. Some people identified more with Peter, some with Mary, some with Barnabas, some with Saul, some with Moses, some with Deborah and some with Jacob—to name only a few of the role-taking options in the Jewish/Christian tradition. Why these differences? Are they purely arbitrary? Are they the chance effects of hearing a specific scripture read, or being inspired by a certain sermon on a given Sunday? Or are their choices related to more enduring characteristics of worshipers themselves which color and shape their ways of being religious?

There is a common-sense adage about behavior that psychologists have reduced to a formula. It goes like this: "B = P + E; Behavior is a function of the Person plus the Environment." Of course, the question always is: "Which is more important, the Person or the Environment?" And, of course the answer always is "both." The religious environment is crucial, as we saw in the case of the boy Samuel in the temple. But the individual is important, too. Samuel became a unique person as a result of the shaping of his personality by Eli. Samuel's religious experience was a function of both the temple environment and his own character. Without implying that the religious environment is unimportant, in this chapter I want to emphasize those unique inside-the-person differences that people bring to the religious environment.

Psychologists call being singularly inspired by a worship

service, as opposed to filtering one's experience of God through one's sex, race, age, or life situation, the difference between "states" and "traits." **States** are those day-to-day moods with which we are all familiar. These states of mind affect our experiences and determine the way things look to us. "States" result from the impact of recent events—those we anticipate and plan and those that accidentally happen and are unexpected. How many times have we, or those we know, returned from religious retreats exhilarated by the inspiration of the event? Religious experience is deeply colored by such times of retreat and worship—be they away from home or special occasions at our parish churches. We speak of these events as "mountain-top" experiences and recognize the difficulties we all have in maintaining religious enthusiasm when we return to the "valleys" of everyday life. Nevertheless, many of us would report that our lives were deeply changed by the **state of mind** which resulted from some experience that overwhelmed us with its impact.

However, it is also true that retreats and special worship occasions affect some people more than others. Not everyone feels inspired to the same degree. This is where **traits** come in. I remember attending worship with my son and daughter-in-law at a Presbyterian church where a woman gave a dramatic reading about Jesus and the woman at the well. I was moved to the point of tears but neither of them were impressed. My son even said that the dramatist sounded like "the witch of the west." He said that he read the church bulletin while she was speaking.

Why this difference in reaction? I suspect it was because of the "traits" each of us brought to the experience. I was a visitor; this was not my church and I didn't know what to expect. This was the church to which my son and daughter-in-law belonged; they were used to a definite pattern of worship which this dramatist disrupted. They filtered their expectations through certain predispositions; one of them may have even been a desire to impress me with what went on at "their" church! Such a story as this illustrates how identifying with such a biblical character as the Samaritan woman-at-the-well could be due as much to what people bring with them as to what happens to them while they are listening to a dramatic reading about her contact with Jesus. These predispositions are called **traits,** by psychologists.

Characteristics such as age, ethnic background, gender, temperament, and/or unique life crises might influence the way in which an experience of God is shaped, interpreted, and applied. Such traits do not change easily, if at all. Certainly, gender and ethnicity are lifelong differences. And, although age changes, it does so slowly, as do many life situations. There are other crisis experiences, such as the divorce of one's parents or debilitating accidents that can have a dramatic impact on personality traits.

Individual temperaments would, likewise, appear to be long-standing and influential. There is widespread agreement among parents who have had more than one child that their children's approach to life varied immensely; such traits as extroversion and introversion can be noticed early in life and seem to be inherited rather than learned. Definitely, traits are more enduring and less susceptible to change than states of mind.

In thinking about why people differ in the ways they are religious, psychologists usually attribute more influence to traits than to states. This can be seen in the very way psychologists label states and traits; states are labeled "states of **mind**" as contrasted with traits which are called "traits of **behavior.**" People's preferences for experiencing God via one or another of the Jewish/Christian dual-role options are differences in religious **behavior.** In fact, most psychologists would contend that most states of mind were dependent on the shape given them by traits. They would further contend that those events which completely overwhelmed persons and short-circuited the influence of their traits were few and far between. Our task in this discussion is look at such traits as sex, age, race, and temperament and see if we can understand how they predetermine why different persons choose and engage in one kind of religious behavior more than another.

Four studies will be discussed. Two of them are theoretical statements about how age and personality effect differences in the experience of religion, and two are research studies of how religious experience is affected by sex and ethnicity.

Personality and Religious Experience

Some years ago, psychologist Paul Barkman suggested that since the Reformation people have been able to choose the type of Christianity to which they will adhere.[1] Although those entering religious orders could select from a number with different emphases, only after the Reformation did the average person have the chance to select from a variety of ways to worship on a given Sunday morning. Barkman contrasted verbal, emotional, social, and transcendental modes of worship and hypothesized that persons tended to gravitate toward the mode that concurred with their dominant personality disposition or trait.

If their basic personality tendencies were to interact verbally or cognitively with the world, Barkman contended that persons might align themselves with Baptist, Reform, Presbyterian or Lutheran churches where correct belief was paramount in importance and where the sermon was the prime focus of worship. If their basic personality tendencies were to interact emotionally or affectively with the world, they might align themselves with Methodists, Assembly of God, Pentecostal or Holiness churches where personal subjective experience was emphasized and emotional expression of inner responses were encouraged. If their basic personality tendencies were to interact socially or interpersonally with the world, they might align themselves with Anabaptists, Disciples of Christ, Mennonite or the United Church of Christ churches where acts of both loving-kindness and social justice were paramount and concerns for social justice were reinforced. If their basic personality tendencies were to interact mystically or transcendentally with the world, they might align themselves with the Episcopal (Anglican), Orthodox, or Roman Catholic churches where the emphasis was placed on the worship service itself, and where private acts of devotion and spirituality were common. It would be easy to suggest specific dual-role paradigms which might fit well into the rational, emotional, social, or spiritual alternatives. Persons within one of these groups might be inclined toward the types of relationships with God which were more aligned with their personality tendencies. Their behav-

ioral **traits** would be grounded in these deep-seated preferences for types of interactions with the world.

However, this model has never been put to a test. Barkman
recognized that it might have been more true for people several centuries ago than at the present time, when urbanization,
geographical distances, and friendship patterns might have significantly compromised the purity of denominational differences. In fact, there may be more personality differences
within churches than **between** them, although the distinctions
Barkman suggests may still be true among those who are most
active in, and identified with, denominational activities above
the local church level. If his model is correct we would expect
to find the differences summarized in the following table:

There is a definite logic to Barkman's model but its validity

---

Table 2-1
The Relation among Personality Traits, Preferred Type of Experiences and Religious Preferences

Personality Tendency	Preferred Experience	Religious Preference
Verbal	beliefs, thoughts (Peter's confession, Mark 8:29)	Calvinists, Lutherans
Emotional	feelings, affects (Disciples on the Emmaus road, Luke 24:13ff)	Pentecostals, Wesleyans
Social	actions, works (The Parable of the Good Samaritan, Luke 10:25ff)	Anabaptists, Liberals
Transcendental	mystery, worship (Isaiah in the Temple, Isaiah 6:1ff)	Catholics, Orthodox

needs to be tested. If proven incorrect, as it well might be, one might wonder to what extent a given parish church should, or should not, take personality differences into consideration in its approach. Perhaps a given church might want to focus in on one of these options and make a special appeal to persons whose traits predetermined that they would respond better to one approach than another. At the very least, a church that provided a variety of types of religious environments might become intentional about designing particular events to appeal to persons with different temperaments. Hopefully, readers will recognize that I did not state any preference for or evaluation of the several options that Barkman listed in his model. Each type of emphasis would seem to me to have a valid place in the Jewish/Christian tradition.

Age and Religious Experience

It does not take special wisdom to acknowledge that for a significant number of people religion has special meaning for them at three times during their life span: at birth, at marriage, and at death. Following ancient traditions, families bring their babies to church for baptism or dedication, their youth to church for marriage, and their loved ones to church for burial. At the very least, religion speaks to their need to honor the miracle of birth, to bless the beauty of loving relationships, and to reassure themselves in the face of the mystery and terror of death. If these events occur normally in the lives of families, they would occur when fathers and mothers were in young adulthood, middle adulthood, and late adulthood; in other words, at different ages. There is probably no parish church that does not offer rituals to meet these needs.

This much is obvious. What is not so obvious, however, are the unique ways in which religion meets persons' individual needs before and after they have dedicated their infants, married their children, and buried their parents. What are the unique religious experiences and needs of children, of adolescents, and of the aged? The theories of Elkind and Erikson speak to these issues.

Psychologist David Elkind[2] contended that religion provides resolutions to the developing cognitive needs of children as they move in four stages from infancy to adolescence. Using the model of Piaget, the Swiss developmental psychologist, Elkind suggested that religion meets persons' needs for conservation, for representation, for relations, and for comprehension.

In infancy, according to Elkind, no accomplishment is more remarkable than the discovery that objects exist even when they are no longer seen, smelled, tasted, or heard. This is called "conservation." Adults have a hard time realizing that infants find this to be a very difficult task. Only after about the second year of life do babies start to cry when mothers leave their cribs. This means they are aware their mothers have left and gone some other place. They realize that their mothers do not cease to exist when they cannot see them; their mothers have simply chosen to leave, but they have not disappeared. They cry so that their mothers will return. This is called **"object permanence."** It is an important prerequisite for all future learning.

In a sense, this search for that which lasts and does not change is a lifelong quest. The words of the hymn, "Abide with Me," attest to this desire: "Change and decay in all about I see/ Oh thou who changest not/Abide with me." Although infants may not extend their quest for object permanence to this ultimate extreme, the foundational answer to their yearning is laid in infancy by ritual acts and faith pronouncements. They are presented at the altar of the church and are told that this, and the love of their parents, symbolizes the unchanging foundation of God's love on which their life is grounded—even before they accord permanence to other parts of their world. They are surrounded, in words and deeds in the best of families, by parents who are stand-ins for this God who is the permanent object par excellence!

It is a truism of developmental psychology that the self-confidence of children to venture out and take the initiative in interacting with the world is based on this deep-seated assurance that parents are always there and that one can always go back to them if there is a need. Religion provides the essential rationale for that confidence by its proclamation that life is encompassed by a God who "neither slumbers nor sleeps" (cf. Psalm 121:4).

Leaving infancy and its search for object permanence, early childhood is characterized by a new cognitive need, the search for **representation**. Representations are words and symbols. During the preschool years, children learn to speak and play in an "as-if" mode. They are able to enter into life indirectly through these signs that stand for realities outside them. They walk in parents' shoes, they play house, they pretend, they draw and they sing. They go in-and-out of "play" houses and assume the roles of fathers, mothers, and children. They mimic adults.

Religiously, these are the years during which children first become aware of the practices and rituals of religion. They are introduced to the Bible and the church as the representations of a God who acts in history and who calls them to respond. They attend worship, bow in prayer, are included in some of the rites, are read to from the Bible, say grace over their meals, and participate in family devotions. They are told that "this is what Christians do because Christ has come, has died, and is resurrected." Their search for representations is met, in part, by incorporation into a tradition with its many symbols, rituals, and requirements. They experience the promise that sometime in the future, when they have made a decision of their own, they will be admitted to the supreme representative acts, the eucharist (Lord's supper) and/or baptism.

Like object permanence, representation is, itself, a cognitive need which will be with children all their lives. They will search for and participate in symbolic acts whereby they make contact with reality. They will even yearn for depth experiences that go beyond their representations. This urge prepares children for the time when they will seek a direct contact with God—a type of personal experience that will make all representations take on a new and deeper meaning.

The third developmental period of childhood pertains to the school years in which the cognitive need is for **relations**. The special skills that children learn during this period are reading and writing. They acquire the desire to relate things to one another through logic and consistency. Sometimes called the "age of reason," this is the time that children begin to think systematically. Youngsters want to know how things work, where they come from, and what they are made of, according to Elkind. Integral to this search is the desire to put things together and, most importantly, to begin to integrate their lives into a larger environment.

Religion offers a ready-made scheme and means for meeting this need for relations in an all-encompassing, comprehensive manner. Through confirmation, or decision, or baptism, or joining the church, children during these pre-pubescent years are afforded a transcendent understanding of their lives. They are provided a set of steps to take which indicates they have made the profound decision to relate themselves to God and his will for life. They reaffirm their relationship to God's creative/redemptive action which was proclaimed by their parents in their baptism/dedication as infants. They experience themselves related to the cosmos and integrated into the will of God for life.

Although the search for relations, like object permanence and representation, is a lifelong endeavor, it has its significant beginning in these religious rituals and dogmas. They provide a foundation for reexperiencing and rededication which serve to rerelate persons to reality again and again throughout their lives. Through bouts of doubt and anxiety, through tragedy and triumph, through health and sickness, through good times and bad, this affirmation of meaning and purpose will provide a foundation for faith that will persist.

The final developmental period prior to adulthood is adolescence. During these years, new mental capacities emerge which enable persons to accomplish feats far surpassing earlier childhood thinking. Adolescents are able to introspect, to idealize and to problem solve in a systematic manner. Their cognitive need is to think **comprehensively**. They yearn to find underlying laws and principles that tie together diverse phenomena.

Once again religion, through its dogmas, its truths, its myths, its beliefs, its rites and its theologies, provides unsurpassed comprehension. A total and encompassing set of assumptions are provided. Adolescents can argue about, dialogue with, apprehend and appropriate these models and reach their own unique conclusions. This is the time of debate during which the worship of the church goes on unabated. Adolescents relate themselves to the church in ambivalent, but often implicitly trusting, ways. Most importantly, religion calls adolescents to invest their lives in a comprehensive scheme which incorporates creation and vocation. They are challenged to give themselves to a cause that will both outlast them and, at the same time, will give meaning to their everyday lives, here and now.

Of course the search for comprehension, like all the preceding cognitive needs, continues throughout life. By responding to this adolescent need in a non-defensive, supportive manner, the church can provide a basis for this pilgrimage which will incorporate, rather than alienate, persons as they move into adulthood.

Elkind's model, based on Piaget's cognitive needs, helps us appreciate how religion addresses unique concerns of persons in the childhood and adolescent years. While it does not provide a basis for predicting which of the dual-role models individuals will choose in their religious experience, it does give pastors a basis for sensing what is going on beneath the surface when they deal with individuals during these life-stages.

Jumping across the young and middle adult years to older adulthood, the psychoanalyst Erik Erikson proposed an understanding of the major need persons have at this time in their lives which relates well to the reassurance religion has to offer.

Erikson[3] suggests that life is composed of a set of "ego-crises" which people face at different stages of their lives. The crisis of older adulthood is **"integrity versus despair."** After persons have passed through the child-rearing and work-production years of life, they retire. During these retirement years they reflect on the way they have lived their lives. Their assessments tend either toward a sense of despair or a sense of integrity.

According to Erikson, those who are satisfied with the way they have lived their lives and would live them over again in the same manner will have the most healthy egos. Their sense of life's integrity will provide them the inner strength to face old age and death. Despair is the lot of those whose reflections cause them to feel that their lives have had little worth. They are deeply frustrated that they have no chance to live life over in a different way.

The Christian tradition meets this need to avoid despair and to affirm integrity. Its message is one of judgment and grace, confrontation and comfort. It preaches both that God will come ". . . to judge the living and the dead," but that there is ". . . the forgiveness of sins." It also challenges the aged to believe that life is not over; there is still time to follow Jesus who "went about doing good" (Acts 10:38). Its gospels tell such parables: The Talents (Luke 19:11ff), the Foolish Virgins (Matthew 25:1ff), the Good Samaritan (Luke 10:25ff) and the Last Judgment (Matthew 25:31ff), as well as the parables of the Unforgiving Servant (Matthew 18:23ff), the Prodigal Son (Luke 15:11ff) and the Laborers in the Vineyard (Matthew 20:1ff), with whom the aged can identify.

The acceptance and steadfast love of God is unquestionably proclaimed to aging persons in the assertion of St. Paul that they can have self-confidence because ". . . by grace you have been saved through faith, and this is not your own doing; it is the gift of God—not the result of works, so that no one may boast" (Ephesians 2:8). Integrity grounded in these truths can overcome the despair of aging persons. This life-stage need of people at this time in life helps us understand when they might tend to fashion their religious experience around such dual-roles as the Prodigal Son and the Last Judgment, in addition to the other options listed above.

Gender and Religious Experience

Turning from personality and age to the trait of gender, the question might be asked: "Do men and women have different kinds of religious experiences?" Many thinkers contend that they do. Deborah Tannen, professor of linguistics at Georgetown University recently stated in an interview about her book, *You Just Don't Understand: Women and Men in Conversation,*[4] that when she analyzed videotaped interviews of boys talking about boys and girls talking about girls she had the feeling that she was looking at two different species.

A number of writers have asserted that Tannen is correct but that society, in general, and religion, in particular, have ignored these differences. Society and religion have acted as if males and females were alike and have tended to design everything on the assumption that men knew what was good for women, according to this point of view. In fact, religion has been accused of being overly patriarchal in its dominance of women by men and in its perpetuation of traditional sex-role differences in its approaches.

If true, the impact of these practices is puzzling because a significant majority of people who are involved in institutional religion are women. If women's needs are not being met, why are they still coming to church? The call of critics for a more androgynous, less male-dominant religion might have the opposite of the intended effect. Fewer, rather than more women, might want to be religious.

Of course, critics have suggested that this could be very healthy since, from their point of view, women need to become aware that they have bought-in to men's judgments about their religious experience. Women need their consciousness raised. Once that happens they will no longer tolerate being religiously dependent and subservient. Unfortunately, many of these ideas have been untested theories. The contention that women's experiences were being violated by male-dominated religious practices had been based on little research until Catherine Smith undertook her study of a group of Protestant women.

Smith surveyed religious experience among a group of church women in southern California. She was interested in how masculine and feminine traits in their perceptions of themselves, in their view of typical men and women, and in their descriptions of what God was like, affected the vitality of their religious experience. While comparing scores on several questionnaires such as these do not give us warrant for stating "what caused what" the results do provide a basis for some hunches about how sex and religion are related.[5]

In studying the effect of education, Smith found that those with more education tended to rate the typical man as less feminine and the typical woman as less masculine. This result is difficult to understand since it is contrary to the expected effect of education. We might have anticipated that those with more education, not less, would have attributed more feminine traits to men and more masculine traits to women—particularly since educated women often are high achievers and achievement has traditionally been conceived as a male-oriented trait.

However, those who were more educated may have been stating that this is the way they saw most people behaving; men being macho, women being demure. If they had been asked what men and women **should** be like, their judgments might have been different.

This possibility can be seen in these women's ratings of themselves. As contrasted with typical women, they judged themselves to be more masculine. Less than 2% of the women pictured themselves as relational, deferring, and passive; i.e., more feminine than masculine. On the contrary, they pictured themselves as assertive, active, and goal-oriented. This tendency to rate themselves as more masculine than the average was different from several previous surveys of Christian women which found them to be more likely to fit the stereotype of being overly-feminine. It could be that the age of women in Smith's study explained this difference. Her women were forty-six years of age on the average while many of the previous studies were conducted on college students.

However, age alone cannot explain the tendency for these women to rate themselves as overly masculine. The women in Smith's study were very active in institutional Christianity; 94% of them attended church weekly. Their self-ratings do not match the passive, dependent picture of women who had become adapted to a subjugating, patriarchal environment. Maybe their religious experience in mainline Protestant Christianity had not been as repressive as some of the critics have predicted it is.

Perhaps organized religion has learned something that the critics have not appreciated. Church leaders in mainline Protestant Christianity have been discussing women's issues for some time. Leaders in this section of the church would have little investment in keeping women in stereotypical supportive roles—quite apart from any continuing discussion over the ordination of women. What we may see in this older group of Christian women could be the result of this decades-long emphasis on the religious empowerment of women.

Smith found one counterindication to this interpretation, however. These women's self-esteem was lower than would have been expected from their ratings of themselves as achieving and assertive. Did their masculine self-identification mean that they unwillingly had sacrificed their femininity and overly conformed to a masculine style of life in order to survive in the church? If this was so, the church would have had no better effect on them than culture—which has tended to overvalue masculine traits, according to most thinkers. The church would be simply reflecting culture; masculine is good, feminine is bad.

It is interesting to note that the small group of women who classified themselves as "undifferentiated" tended to be those with the highest self-esteem. Undifferentiated persons have been thought to be those who have not made up their minds about their self-perceptions. Often this has been correlated with lower self-esteem. The opposite tendency of undifferentiated women in this study to rate themselves as higher in self-esteem is puzzling, unless it reflects a willingness to remain flexible and comfortable in not fully knowing what one's role shall be, because of confidence in the grace of God that sustained them in this struggle. This is an inference that needs further investigation.

Of major concern in the Smith study, however, was how these issues related to the women's concepts of God and to the vitality of their religious experiences. When described in terms of masculine and feminine traits, the women's concepts of God were more similar to their perceptions of themselves than was true in a group of men's self and God perceptions, which was also studied. This was contrary to what had been predicted, since the critics had suggested that men, but not women, would be able to identify with the Jewish/Christian God who, these critics contended, had always been described in masculine terms.

Smith had predicted that where self and God descriptions were more alike, religious experience would be more vital. Unfortunately, this was not true. Although these women reported a high level of intensity and vitality in their religious experiences, these ratings did not tend to be related to those who rated their traits as more similar to their descriptions of God. Furthermore, more intense religious vitality was not related to more positive self-esteem.

So what conclusions can we make on the basis of Smith's study about whether gender differences provoke or influence religious experiences? In spite of the logic that being male or female should affect religious experience, Smith's study offers no support for this hypothesis. Something other than differences between the sexes seems to be operating.

Of course, there are limits to this study. The sample was geographically limited and did not cover all differences among Christian traditions. Yet, if the results be generalized, we can say that while church women seem to not be as subservient and passive as they have been in the past, this new-found assertion does not seem to have increased their self-esteem nor does it seem related to the vitality of their experience of God. Contrary to what had been presumed, however, women seem to be able to identify with God; their self-perceptions are more similar to their God-perceptions than men's. Much more work needs to be done on how being religious is related to sexual differences and this study is a good example of how important it is not to oversimplify the issues.

Race and Religious Experience

Race or "ethnicity" is yet another trait that might affect different ways of being religious. This affect may be seen in cultural preferences for ways of worshiping. Black gospel singing is easily distinguishable from white formal hymn singing. Research conducted in the 1960s and 1970s found that blacks were more likely to hold traditional religious beliefs, to attend religious services more often, to report having had a religious experience and to rate religion more important in their lives than were whites. In the 1980s, Philip Pannell undertook a survey to see whether these differences still existed.

Pannell compared a sample of Michigan and California black Christians to national samples of whites on answers they gave to a well-known measure of religious dimensions. This measure, called the King and Hunt Scales, assesses the following twelve ways of being religious. It is reprinted, with permission, in the Appendix and can be used by pastors with their congregations.

1. Creedal Assent—agreement with doctrinal orthodoxy
2. Devotionalism—personal prayer and closeness to God
3. Church Attendance—frequency of worship
4. Organizational Activity—participation and satisfaction in church work
5. Financial Support—percent of income given to church
6. Religious Knowledge—awareness of theological and historical issues
7. Orientation to Growth and Striving—continued attempts to find out what God wants in life
8. Extrinsic Motivation—seeing religion as serving one's need for friendship, fellowship, and self-protection
9. Salience: Behavior—the importance of religious behavior
10. Salience: Cognition—the importance of religious beliefs and thinking
11. Social Action—seeing the church as an agent of social change
12. Personal Service—being involved in helping others.

In his comparison of black and white ways of being religious,[6] Pannell found that blacks scored higher than whites on Creedal Assent, Devotionalism, Organizational Activity, Extrinsic Motivation, Salience: Behavior, Salience: Cognition, Social Action and Personal Service. Whites scored higher than blacks on Church Attendance, Financial Involvement, and Religious Knowledge.

The results of Pannell's study are interesting; they confirm the earlier studies. Although they do not clarify which of the dual-role alternatives would appeal more to blacks than to whites, they do suggest a difference in styles that makes sense in light of past cultural and socio-economic realities in America.

It is understandable why whites would give more money to the church and have greater religious knowledge than blacks in light of the educational and financial advantages that they have enjoyed. Moreover, it is understandable why blacks would show greater concern for social justice and be motivated more extrinsically than whites because of the more central role the church continues to play in black culture and because of the past social injustice blacks have experienced.

The most puzzling aspect of Pannell's findings was that whites' church attendance was greater, but that blacks' organizational activity was higher. It could be inferred that whites' participation was more formal and ritual but that blacks' participation was more social and functional. This difference needs to be investigated further and its import for church life needs to be explored.

Conclusion

This chapter has tried to show some of the more enduring traits that people bring to their religious experience. Since we know that there are many ways to be religious, the question is: "Do personal traits, such as age, race, sex, and temperament, shape and color the manner in which faith is received and expressed?" Although not all possible individual differences have been considered in this chapter, the ones that have been discussed are among the more important.

Three theories and two research studies were described. Barkman's suggestion that people's temperamental preferences for approaching life in a verbal, emotional, social, and transcendental style determined their choices of different Christian churches is provocative, but untested. Elkind's model for the ways that religion can meet children's and adolescents' needs has had much import for religious education. Erikson's contention that the ego-crisis of old age is to achieve the virtue of integrity can easily guide the care that pastors give persons at this time in their lives. Smith's study of women revealed that the relationship between sex and religious experience is not as simple and straightforward as has been presumed. Finally, Pannell's comparison of black and white ways of being religious evidenced some crucial differences that could be considered when planning church programs.

I turn next to the question of religious maturity. It is one thing to describe differences in religious behavior; it is another thing to make a value judgment about whether one way of being religious is better than another. There is much talk today about becoming more "spiritual." For at least two centuries there has been talk about "growth in grace," "sanctification" and "the blessing of the Holy Spirit." What have psychologists found out about growth in religion? Is there such a thing as mature religion? This the topic to which we now turn.

For Further Reading

James W. Fowler, *Stages of Faith: The Psychology of Human Development and the Quest for Meaning* (San Francisco: Harper & Row, 1981).

Don Browning, "Faith and the Dynamics of Knowing," in *The Dialogue between Theology and Psychology*, ed. Peter Homans (Chicago: University of Chicago Press, 1968), p. 26ff.

Chapter 3

Really Believing: Is There Such a Thing as Mature Religion?

In the previous two chapters, I have been **describing** religion; now, I want to **evaluate** it. Description is one thing; evaluation is another. For example, consider the report of differences in black and white ways of being religious reported in the last chapter. Blacks scored higher than whites on some measures and whites scored higher than blacks on others. They were different but was one way of being religious better than the others? Maybe the best, or most mature, way of being religious would be to score high on all the measures; higher than either the blacks or whites! This possibility leads us into the topic of this chapter, namely, "What is mature religion? What does it mean to **really** believe and to practice one's faith in an optimal manner?"

Defining Religious Maturity

There are two ways to define maturity. One way is internal, the other is external. Both are idealistic in that they describe how something would look if it were functioning perfectly. Take a building crane, for example. Internally, the crane would be "mature" if all its parts were functioning harmoniously and all its motors responding faultlessly to operator commands. Externally, the crane would be "mature" if it picked up materials from off the ground, lifted them up and then deposited them high on the scaffolding of the building—flawlessly and smoothly. One definition focuses on the internal workings of the crane while the other definition focuses on the tasks that cranes are built to accomplish.

Religious maturity is similar. It, too, can be understood internally and externally. Jesus included both in his answer to the question, "What is the first and great commandment?" He responded, "The first is, 'Hear, O Israel: the Lord our God, the Lord is one; you shall love the Lord with all your heart, and with all your soul, and with all your mind, and with all your strength' (an internal definition). The second is this, 'You shall love your neighbor as yourself'" (an external definition). "There is no other commandment greater than these" (Mark 12:28–31). Loving God with all one's heart, soul, mind, and strength is something one does **inside** religion through beliefs, worship, rituals, practices. Loving one's neighbor as oneself is something one does **outside** religion through kindness, justice, compassion, and assistance. This short statement of Jesus is a comprehensive description of mature religion.

Thus, optimal religious functioning can be understood in a similar manner to optimally functioning mature building cranes; internally and externally. The turn of the century psychologist of religion, William James, called these two aspects of religion, religion's "roots" and religion's "fruits." The biblical writer of the book of James labeled these two aspects of religion religion's "faith" and religion's "works." Noting that both are necessary, James concluded, "So faith by itself, if it has no works, is dead" (3:17).

More recently, Gordon Allport proposed a sixfold definition of mature religion which combined both internal and external dimensions.[1] He suggested mature religion is:

1. **Well Differentiated**—Mature religion has been well thought out and includes many different facets. This is an "internal" emphasis.

2. **Dynamic in Character in Spite of its Derivative Nature**—Mature religion meets present, real needs even though it may have originated in childhood and it may represent accommodation to one's family and culture. This is an "internal" emphasis.

3. **Productive of a Consistent Morality**—Mature religion provokes ethical concerns and produces moral behavior as well

as a concern for values in both personal and social relationships. This is an "external" emphasis.

4. **Comprehensive**—Mature religion provides a "master motive" for all of life. This includes both an "internal" and "external" emphasis.

5. **Integral**—Mature religion stimulates self-reflection and has relevance for all aspects of one's personality. This is an "internal" emphasis.

6. **Heuristic**—Mature religion is always open to new ideas and to new applications; it tolerates doubt and stimulates growth. This is an "external" emphasis.

Later, Allport incorporated these facets of mature religion into twofold distinction between Intrinsic and Extrinsic religion. He concluded that Extrinsic religious persons **use** their religion while Intrinsic religious persons **live** theirs. Obviously, he felt that Intrinsic religion was more mature than Extrinsic religion.

This distinction has been widely investigated by psychologists during the last thirty years. Although in a number of studies, such as who would be more racially prejudiced, Extrinsics have appeared less mature than Intrinsics, the results have not always been as predicted.[2] Nevertheless, assessing persons on whether their approaches to religion are more Extrinsically or Intrinsically oriented is still a helpful thing to do. In the Appendix to this book is the "Age-Universal I-E Scale,"[3] developed by psychologists Richard Gorsuch and Dan Venable, that can be used by pastors in spiritual guidance and counseling to help people become more aware of their spiritual maturity.

One difficulty with Allport's definitions of religious maturity is that they emphasize style but not content. The Intrinisic-Extrinsic distinction could apply to any religion. While, as a psychologist, I do not mean to suggest that the Christian faith is better than any other religion, although that may be true, I do think that there is a need to look more deeply into what religious maturity looks like from **within** Christianity itself. To do this we need to look not only at how specific Christian beliefs function in daily living, but also at the Intrinsic or Extrinsic styles of being religious. Considering beliefs as well as styles as being important in defining religious maturity was emphasized by psychologist Paul Pruyser, to whose thinking we now turn.

Pruyser's Model of Religious Maturity

While Pruyser was a psychologist at the Menninger Foundation he proposed a model for understanding religious maturity based on how well persons were applying Christian **beliefs** to their daily lives. In his work at this well-known psychiatric center, he noted that the hospital chaplains tended to use psychological terms in describing patients at case conferences. He concluded that the time-honored teachings of the religious traditions about abundant, or mature, living were being ignored by the chaplains. Instead, they were using psychological jargon to report their findings.

When chaplains ignored the beliefs of the patients, Pruyser felt that the **content** of religion was being bypassed. He suggested that if the chaplains were to use religious terms to report on the spiritual conditions of the hospital patients, their judgments might be just as valuable as the reports of the psychologists, the psychiatrists, and the social workers. Pruyser recalled that, after all, religion has been thinking about the good life for a long time. He concluded that lack of the "abundant life," which Jesus promised (cf. John 10:10), might be due to people's spiritual condition just as much as to their emotional, mental and social conditions. How they were applying their religious beliefs might be just as important for their sickness or health as anything else in their lives. It was his strong opinion that the founders of all religions intended that beliefs should be put into practice and that happiness, joy, and adjustment would be the result.

What was needed, according to Pruyser, was a method of assessing the **content** as well as the **application** of beliefs. He proposed that chaplains interview patients about how they were applying eight religious beliefs to their daily lives. These are as follows:[4]

1. **Awareness of God**—The more people experience a sense of awe and creatureliness in relation to God, the more mature their religion would be.

2. **Acceptance of God's Grace and Steadfast Love**—The more people understand and experience God's benevolence and unconditional love and acceptance, the more mature their religion would be.

3. **Being Repentant and Responsible**—The more people take responsibility for their own feelings and behavior, the more mature their religion would be.

4. **Knowing God's Leadership and Direction**—The more people trust in, hope for, and live out God's guidance in their lives, the more mature their religion would be.

5. **Involvement in Organized Religion**—The more people are involved quantitatively, qualitatively and motivationally in the church, the more mature their religion would be.

6. **Experiencing Fellowship**—The more people relate meaningfully with others and the greater their sense of interpersonal identification, the more mature their religion would be.

7. **Being Ethical**—The more people are committed to the application of ethical principles in their lives, the more mature their religion would be.

8. **Affirming Openness in Faith**—The more people are growing, elaborating and being open to newness in their faith, the more mature their religion would be.

Pruyser's approach is a good combination of internal and external definitions of maturity. It combines faith with work. Although it focuses on behaviors, it does not ignore the fact that **what** they believe is the foundation for **how** they behave. In contrast to William James, who said he was more interested in the fruits, or results, of religion than its roots, or origins, Pruyser's model includes a concern for both roots and fruits. Nevertheless, this balance of internal and external emphases does not equate verbal statements of belief; i.e., creedal orthodoxy, with mature faith. Pruyser's dimensions pertain to the **application** of beliefs, not just their affirmation. The key difference lies in what occurs between repeating the words of a creed on Sunday and the utilization of those beliefs in how one lives the rest of the week. How theology "functions" is the issue.

Pruyser's model is very similar to Allport's in a number of ways. The significant difference is that Pruyser's model is tradition-specific and takes seriously the content of Christian teachings about religious maturity while Allport's does not. In fact, instead of "religious maturity," terms which better describe what Pruyser had in mind, might be "optimal Christian living" or "functional theology."

Christian Uniqueness

It is important to note the obvious: Pruyser's approach assumes that the teachings of the Christian church, its theology, underlie abundant living. Those who are aware of God in his creative, redemptive, and sustaining power, who experience his acceptance and love, who are aware of their failures yet know they are forgiven, who are forgiving and responsible, who look to God for guidance, who are part of the church, who work for justice in relationships and in society, and who remain open to newness and are tolerant of others—these are mature Christians; their beliefs are functioning for them.

Expressed in theological terms, these mature Christians are those who have identity, integrity, and inspiration.

They have **identity** in that their self-understanding is that they are children of God—created by him and destined to live according to a divine plan.

They have **integrity** in that their daily lives are lived in the awareness that they have been redeemed by God's grace from the guilt of alienation, anxiety and sin and that they can freely respond to God's will in the present.

They have **inspiration** in that they live with the sense that God is available to sustain, comfort, encourage, challenge, and direct their lives on a daily basis.

These aspects of Christian religious maturity relate to beliefs in God the Father, God the Son, and God the Holy Spirit. They pertain to the Christian doctrines of creation, redemption, and sanctification. They provide the foundation for practical daily living.[5]

That is why Pruyser's model and this elaboration of its meaning can be labeled "functional theology." Using "functional theology" as a synonym for "religious maturity" keeps us mindful of the fact that the vast majority of people are religious within the structures of a traditional religion, and that their religious maturity must be judged from within the particular religion they espouse. As we noted in the first chapter, religious traditions provide handles whereby people can make contact with God in ways that give meaning and engender social support. There are very few religious isolates. That is the reason that Pruyser's model is preferable to Allport's. It does not assume that beliefs can all be subsumed under psychological categories and/or Intrinsic and Extrinsic religious styles.

In the western world, the dominant religious tradition is the Christian faith. This is the tradition Pruyser knew best. It is the one around which his approach is designed. I think he would encourage psychologists who knew the other great religious traditions to think through what religious maturity meant from within their points of view.

However, since the concern of most readers of this book is the Christian ministry, it behooves us to be reminded of the unique assumptions on which that faith is based. A list of these is given below. Christianity is:

theistic—it believes there is a divine being;

revelational—it believe this divine being has made himself known through inspired writings and through his Son, Jesus the Christ;

historical—it believes that history (natural and human) is the arena in which God's will has been revealed and is to be accomplished;

transactional—it believes that the will of God is for persons to do something good and worthy with their time and energy;

ethical—it believes that life is to be guided by the principles of justice and love;

interpersonal—it believes that the will of God is primarily, but not exclusively, concerned with how people live together;

corporate—it believes that the church stands in the tradition of the Hebrew people, the temple and the synagogue and is the foremost witness to God's presence in the world and the prime means through which faith is to be nurtured and expressed; and

eschatological—it believes that God has a final purpose for all of history with which persons are called to identify and the hope of which they are to live.

It should be obvious that not all of these assumptions are absolutely unique to Christianity. Several of them are shared with Judaism and Islam, for example. But the combination of them and their central affirmation that Jesus is God's messiah, grounds Christian religious maturity on a foundation that is novel, to say the least. These presumptions cannot be ignored when defining religious maturity.

A Way to Measure "Functional Theology"

The Religious Status Interview: Pruyser was a psychologist. He was not only interested in developing a model; he was also interested in designing a means by which hospital chaplains and parish pastors could make judgments about religious maturity. He wanted pastors to be able to make religious "diagnoses." In fact, he titled his book on this subject *The Minister as Diagnostician*. He died before his ideas could be put into a definite format.

However, my students and I have developed a set of thirty-three questions which can be used by pastors to fulfill Pruyser's dream. It is called the **Religious Status Inventory**,[6] and contains the following: six questions about Awareness of God; four questions about Acceptance of God's Grace and Steadfast Love; five questions about Being Repentant and Responsible; three questions about Knowing God's Leadership and Direction; four questions about Involvement in Organized Religion; three questions about Experiencing Fellowship; four questions about Being Ethical and four questions about Openness in Faith. A copy of these questions is included in the Appendix of this book.

It will be noticed that the answers people give to each

question are rated on a 1- to 5-point scale, so that if persons were rated as totally religiously mature, they will obtain a score of 165 (5 times 33), and if they were rated as totally immature, they will obtain a score of 33 (1 times 33). After each question, statements are provided to help pastors make these judgments about the people's answers to the questions.

Examples of the questions and the ratings are given below:

Question 24 (under Experiencing Fellowship: Identification as a Child of God):

"What does being part of the family of God mean to you?"

Ratings: Give the answer

1—if this person expresses a sense of exclusiveness in his/her identity with the family of God or displays a self-righteous, judgmental attitude or condemns others who express their faith differently;

2—an answer judged to be between 1 and 3;

3—if this person's identity with the family of God includes some sense of superiority over those who seem to be outside the family of God;

4—an answer judged to be between 3 and 5;

5—if this person identifies positively with the family of God, yet this includes a sense of community with the "people of God" everywhere and has an attitude of humble appreciation for salvation.

Question 14 (under Being Repentant and Responsible: Requesting Forgiveness):

"What do you do when you have wronged someone?"

Ratings: Give the answer a

1—if this person completely denies or rationalizes any need to ask for forgiveness from another person;

2—an answer judged to be between 1 and 3;

3—if this person seldom asks for forgiveness;

4—an answer judged to be between 3 and 5;

5—if this person is able to request and accept forgiveness from others without feeling threatened or self-depreciating;

4—an answer judged to be between 5 and 3;

3—if this person has some difficulty accepting forgiveness from others;

2—an answer judged to be between 3 and 1;

1—if this person asks for forgiveness, but is unable to accept it or feels very unworthy of receiving forgiveness.

It will be noticed that the first example included ratings which were along a 1 to 5 continuum, but that the second example's rating involved 1 to 5 to 1. This is because in some cases the answers can be rated in a straightforward "less to more" fashion, while in other cases a balance between two extremes is rated more highly. In the first example, answers which reflected a clear identification of oneself as God's child but which at the same time showed a tolerance for persons whose ways of being Christian might differ, were considered more mature than those who were self-righteous and judgmental of others. However, in the second example, higher maturity ratings were given those who could both ask for and receive forgiveness, than persons who saw no need to ask forgiveness or who could not accept it when they asked for it. There are eleven questions whose ratings reflect a need for balance between extremes; the other twenty-two question-ratings are based on less to more of a given quality.

Ministers are encouraged to use these questions and ratings to counsel people who are having difficulties about how to grow in their religious maturity and apply their faith to their daily lives. In addition, these questions can be used in spiritual direction, as persons seek to increase their maturity. There are no norms against which persons can compare their scores. The numbers should be used as guidelines for areas in which persons can grow in their faith. However, pastors should avoid using the numbers to classify people as "mature" or "immature" in any authoritative, punitive manner.

The Religious Status Inventory: In addition to the Interview questions described above we have developed a paper-and-pencil questionnaire which can be used when there is not enough time for extensive interviewing or when people want to get a quick look at their religious maturity. We designed the Inventory along the same lines as the Interview.[7] All of Pruyser's eight dimensions are assessed. The Inventory is composed of 160 statements to which persons respond as "Not true of me" or "True of me" along a 1- to 5-point scale. Examples of the statements on the Inventory are given below:

No. 94. "My faith affects every aspect of my life" (Openness in Faith).

No. 100. "Pain makes me question God's role in my life" (Acceptance of God's Grace and Steadfast Love).

No. 72. "I volunteer quite often for church positions" (Involvement in Organized Religion).

No. 80. "I would lose interest in my job if it paid less" (Being Ethical).

No. 20. "God can use my anger in positive ways" (Being Repentant and Responsible).

No. 3. "Making a decision is as simple as praying to God and waiting for an answer" (Knowing God's Leadership and Direction).

Higher scores reflect greater religious maturity. If persons were to judge themselves completely mature on the Inventory, they would receive a score of 800 (160 times 5), whereas if they were to rate themselves as totally immature, they would receive a score of 160 (160 times 1).

This scoring procedure needs to be corrected in one way, however.

Take a look at questions 100, 80, and 3 above. These statements don't appear to characterize a mature person. They look like the opposite—very immature; and so they are. The Inventory is constructed so that one-half of the statements, for example, number 80, are worded immaturely. If persons rated these statements as "True of me" they would be indicating they were *im*mature, not mature, and the scoring would confound the meaning of the Inventory if it was just added to the total. So, ratings on these scores are reversed. Where persons give themselves 5s, they should be reversed and given 1s; 4s should become 2s and 3s would remain the same. The scoring key attached to the Inventory in the Appendix of this book shows how to do this.

As with the Interview, there are no norms for the Inventory. Each person should be treated individually and uniquely. When using the Inventory, ministers should share the scores with those they are counseling or directing and use them in conversations about how to increase the application of faith to daily lives. Again, they should avoid typing persons as "mature" or "immature" too easily.

Conclusion

This chapter has dealt with definitions and assessments of religious maturity. As contrasted with other understandings of religious maturity, such as the Intrinsic/Extrinsic model of Allport and the Faith Development theory of James Fowler,[8] Paul Pruyser's "functional theology" approach was described as preferable.

Pruyser's approach avoids a content-less emphasis on religious style (Allport) and an exclusively cognitive emphasis on religious belief (Fowler) in favor of a focus on how beliefs are applied in daily life. Pruyser's eight dimensions have been used in designing both the Religious Status Interview and the Religious Status Inventory. These measures are tradition-specific in that they provide guidelines for how Christian persons are utilizing their convictions in both their internal self-understandings and their external dealings with others. These measures have been found to discriminate among parishioners whom clergy judged to be more or less mature. They are included in the Appendix and can be used by ministers in counseling and in spiritual guidance.

For Further Reading

William James, *The Varieties of Religious Experience* (New York: Mentor, 1902, 1958).

H. Newton Malony, *Understanding Your Faith: A Christian Psychologist Helps You Look at Your Religious Experiences* (Nashville, TN: Abingdon, 1978). Out of print, available from the author.

Chapter 4

Religion and Morals: Does Faith Make Better Persons?

Since the 1930s psychologists have been studying the relationship between religion and morals. The results have been mixed. Sometimes being religious has been found to be correlated with ethical behavior while, at other times, it has not. In their book on the psychology of religion, Spilka, Hood and Gorsuch described several studies on cheating that have been conducted during this century.[1] In an early survey of 11,000 schoolchildren, no association between churchgoing and honesty was demonstrated. In this same study a positive relationship between attendance at Protestant Sunday Schools and less cheating disappeared when social class differences were taken into consideration. A later study of 3,000 children confirmed these relationships. Amount of biblical knowledge had no effect on whether one cheated or not. Studies of college students led to further doubt that religion and morality were associated. Less cheating on examinations was not related to religiousness. While 92% of religious students agreed that cheating was wrong, 87% of them also agreed with the statement: "If everyone else cheats, why shouldn't I?" and 72% confessed that they had actually done so.

These findings are troubling. We typically think that religion should make individuals better persons. Becoming religious should have an effect on how one lives. Religious people **should** be more moral. Of course, being ethical encompasses much more than cheating on tests. Morality has as much to do with the good that one does as well as the bad that one does not do. This chapter will describe three studies that deal with these broader issues. The first study deals with differences in the assumptions that religious persons use when making moral judgments. The second study deals with the impact of situational and religious issues on the likelihood that people will help others who are in trouble. The third study deals with the influence that trying to do what Jesus would do has on self-denial. The conclusions of these studies are both encouraging and discouraging. At the end of the chapter, I will suggest some ways that ministers can use these findings to stimulate and encourage morality in their parishioners.

Making Moral Judgments

Using a scale to measure Lawrence Kohlberg's theories about moral development, Donald Hoagland compared groups of persons across the span of theological positions ranging from fundamentalist to atheist.[2] Harvard educator, Lawrence Kohlberg, contended that the earliest type of moral reasoning in children was "preconventional"—that is, they considered their own self-interests paramount when making decisions about how to behave. At times, such preconventional behavior might appear sacrificial but, at all times, the reasoning beneath preconventional behavior would be selfish. So, for example, when brothers are quarreling over a toy, one might proclaim, "But the ball is mine and I want to play with it!"

This first stage in moral development is called **preconventional** because at the second stage, people conform to convention or custom. And convention is always a society's way of trying to guarantee fairness or "the greatest good for the greatest number." During this "conventional" stage, individuals adjust their behavior to some sort of social contract whereby they reason that "to maximize my own good, I must give up some of my immediate wishes and be concerned with others." Shared interests and expectations make persons become group conscious. Still, however, the main focus is pragmatic and self-centered. So, for example, in the case of the brothers arguing over who should play with a given toy, an older child might say, "I'll let him play with my ball, if he will let me play with his gun."

The third stage in moral development, according to Kohlberg, is termed "principled" because at this stage rational people base their thinking on moral principles on which a just society should be based. Their behavior reflects this concern to act out their essential convictions. Principled action is less concerned with selfishness or unselfishness and more concerned with basic tenets about justice and morality, i.e., ethical principles. So, to extend the toy example one step farther, an adolescent might state, "I'll let him have the ball; it's not right that one person should have many toys and another person have none."

In his study, Hoagland compared attendees at a fundamentalist seminary, an evangelical college, a liberal seminary, a metaphysically oriented church and college, and an atheist society and convention. When he combined the following measures into a composite called "religiousness," Hoagland found that being more religious related positively to conventional and negatively to principled moral reasoning. These measures of religiousness were:

1) belief in God; 2) having been "born again"; 3) being a member of the "Moral Majority"; 4) considering religion to be important in life; 5) being active in both individual and group religious practices; 6) believing that the Bible and Christian theology were literally true; and 7) maintaining a fundamentalist belief system. These criteria were weighted toward the more conservative end of the theological continuum. As expected, those persons who were from these groups tended to score highest on these measures.

This study leads to the conclusion that the more religiously conservative people are, the more likely they are to support conventional, rather than principled, morality. They associate their religious convictions with support for culture's rules for what is right and good.

In a way, this should not be surprising. Religion is always a conserving force in society. It tends to maintain morality and rules of order. There is a subtle temptation for religion to perceive peaceful social functioning as evidence of the blessing of God. Social historians have noted the tendency, at least in western society, for Christianity to reach an accommodation with culture and for society to reflect basically religious convictions in its laws and norms.

Hopefully, Christianity would have had some impact on society and laws, and customs should reflect that influence. However, most religious leaders would like to suppose that religiousness would evoke critique, as well as support, of culture. This prophetic dimension in the Jewish/Christian tradition has always been considered essential. As theologian Julian Hartt suggested in his book, *A Christian Critique of American Culture:*[3] "Christian criticism is founded on the presence of God transcendent in the actual world. . . ." "So far as he [sic] is faithful, the Christian believes that the demands of the righteous God revealed in Jesus Christ transcend every value system. Criticism of the values he shares with the age in which he lives is part of his service offered to his Lord. . . ." ". . . man [sic] is not a mere creature of the social order in which he finds himself."

If Hoagland's results can be generalized, there seems to be a tendency for those who are more law-abiding and critical of deviance to also be those who are more religiously conservative. We do not know whether the opposite is true; i.e., whether the more religiously liberal are more critical of their culture. We do know that they tend to reason in a manner that is based more on ethical principles than on social customs of law and order. The implications of these conclusions for religious education of both youth and adults are important. The balance between adherence to law and order at the same time that one remains reflective and critical is integral to the task of Christian living day-to-day.

Determinants of Helping Those in Need

Turning from research on moral reasoning to the determinants of helping those in need, psychologists John Darley and Daniel Batson assessed the likelihood that a group of Princeton Seminary students would stop to help a disheveled figure lying slumped down along the path when they were going from one building to another. Using the parable of the Good Samaritan

(Luke 10:25ff), these researchers attempted to see whether these students would be more like the priest and Levite in the biblical account who "passed by" or the Samaritan who stopped and gave help to the person in need.[4]

The disheveled person was a helper in the study. He was not really hurt or in need. He was simply playing the part of a semi-comatose person slumped down on the ground. As the seminary students passed by he judged their helpfulness along a five-point scale. He gave a "1" to those who passed by without offering any help and gave a "5" to those who stopped and insisted on taking him for help even when he told them he could take care of himself. All others he rated 2, 3, or 4 depending on the amount of help they did or did not give.

Since all of the students were preparing for the ministry, it was assumed that they were motivated to act religiously. However, prior to moving from one building to another they completed several paper-and-pencil measures of religiosity and were divided into two groups. One group was asked to prepare extemporaneous speeches on either "what makes a good minister" or "the Good Samaritan." They were instructed to think about these speeches as they walked to another campus building where they would be asked to deliver them. Just before they left, half of the students were told to hurry because they were late and the other half were not given any such instruction.

Since these were students preparing for the ministry, it would naturally have been predicted that they would be more inclined to offer help than had they been laypersons. However, the study provided no way to make this comparison, but did provide a way to make other comparisons. It would have been expected that thinking about the story of the Good Samaritan would have had some effect on these students. Being instructed to prepare to give a speech on the Good Samaritan ought to have inclined these students to stop and help because of what was in the forefront of their minds—regardless of whether they were in a hurry or not. But this was not so. There was no difference in the two groups. Although 59% of the Good Samaritan speakers stopped, 29% of the Good Minister group also stopped and this difference was not statistically significant.

However, those students whose beliefs were more doctrinally orthodox did stop more often than those whose beliefs were less orthodox. The major finding was that not being told to hurry resulted in a greater inclination to stop and offer help. The desire to not be late provoked students to rush by without helping regardless of whether they were going to speak on the "Good Samaritan" or "What makes a good minister."

This research was an ingenious attempt to replicate a biblical story under controlled conditions. The results are troublesome. We would like to think that religious faith makes persons rise above social expectations. Under the stress of the custom of being on time, the ethics of stopping to help a needy person faded away. As in the parable, the same circumstance that determined the behavior of the priest and Levite was the dominant factor here, i.e., being in a hurry. Social expectations overwhelmed professional roles, preparing for the ministry, as well as the mental set of being asked to think about the parable of the Good Samaritan.

The influence of doctrinal orthodoxy on helping others suggests that adherence to doctrine may be more important than states of mind, i.e., whether one has been asked to think about a given biblical passage or not. If one associates doctrinal orthodoxy with religious conservatism, the difference between this study and Hoagland's survey on moral reasoning, reviewed earlier, requires some reflection. Had Hoagland's results been used to make a prediction in this Good Samaritan study, we would probably have not hypothesized that doctrinal orthodoxy would be related to stopping to help, but it was. How can this be explained?

One possibility is that the Good Samaritan study shows what people **actually** do while the Hoagland study only measured what they **say** they would do. It is true that one study assessed behavior while the other study simply related two paper-and-pencil tests. However, it should also be said that the connection between believing in the basic dogmas of Christianity does not seem to be related explicitly to helping others in need **unless** one assumes that underneath those beliefs lies a host of other affirmations such as is integral to such eighth-century prophets as Amos, Jesus' Sermon on the Mount, and the teachings of Paul in such passages as the thirteenth chapter of 1 Corinthians. These assumptions are unstated, however, and would need to be investigated.

How can ministers insure that faith will be deep enough to predict that when there is a need people will stop to meet it regardless of whether or not they are in a hurry? Moreover, there may be a relationship between deeply-held convictions about dogma and helping others that needs to be emphasized and explored in plans for religious education.

Self-Denial and Assuming the Role of Jesus

The third study I would like to describe was an investigation of whether assuming the role of Jesus would have any effect on self-sacrificial behavior. In answering the question of whether religion makes persons more ethical, this chapter has considered cheating behavior, making moral judgments and helping persons in need. Now we turn to a related ethical issue, namely, denying oneself in situations where one could be selfish. Psychologist Richard Raney investigated this question among a group of Christian college students who were instructed to play a game in which they could win chances on a drawing for $100.[5] The students had been selected because of their scores on a test of self-esteem. Half were high and half were low.

In the game, each student was paired with another "student," who was actually a confederate of the experimenter. The game was designed so that, upon a signal from the experimenter, each player held up a blue or red chip. On the basis of a predesigned schedule of payoffs, mounted on a board so all could see, players were given white chips after each move in the game. Players were told that they could later exchange these chips for chances on the $100 drawing.

For example, for times when each player held up a blue chip, player A received 2 chips and player B lost 2 chips, but when each player held up a red chip the reverse was true. When one player held up blue and the other red, player A received 1 chip and player B lost 1, but when the chips were reversed, the payoffs were also reversed.

The schedules of payoffs were so designed that player **A** (the **real** student) could take advantage of the game and win many more white chips than player **B** (the confederate). It was also designed so that whenever player **A** (the **real** student), played the "blue" chip, the other player tended to win; i.e., received more white chips. Knowing that the more chips they won the greater would be their chance of winning the $100 provided an incentive to the students to win as often as they could. Since the **real** student could determine the outcome, because of the way the payoffs were rigged, it was possible to see when he or she was being selfish or self-denying.

The game was played 120 times. Halfway through, at the end of 60 trials, students were given a different mind-set. They were told to play the rest of the game (the next 60 times) as they thought Christ would play it. To control for any influence of the order, half of the students had been instructed to play the first 60 trials as they thought Christ would play the game. They were then told to play the last 60 times to win as much as they could for themselves. The difference in the number of white chips the students had at the end of 60 trials under the two different conditions was thought to be an indication of how much influence assuming the role of Christ would have on self-sacrifice.

As expected, Raney found that when told to assume the Christ role, students were, indeed, more self-denying. They played their blue chips more often, which tended to give more white chips to the other player and fewer white chips to themselves. They won fewer white chips than when instructed to gain as much as they could.

The order in which they were instructed to play the "Christ" role also had an effect. When they started the game assuming the Christ role, they won fewer white chips in the second part of the game than when the Christ role came second. This indicated that remembering their self-sacrifice in the Christ role tempered their later selfishness.

Most importantly, the high self-esteem students were more sacrificial in the Christ role than the low self-esteem students, regardless of whether they played this role before or after the period in which they were trying to win all they could for themselves.

Contrary to the Good Samaritan study described earlier, this research suggested that the religious mental set with which persons approach a situation can influence their behavior. Keeping the image of Christ in their minds did affect their behavior in a way that preparing a speech on the Good Samaritan did not seem to do. However, it should be noted that there was no contradictory social expectation, such as being told to hurry, imposed on them during the event. The pressure to win chances on the drawing was a purely personal motivation. No one would criticize them if they lost nor would they be criticized if they did not act fast enough. We do not know how they would have reacted had they been put into a conflicting social situation. The results also suggest that self-esteem interacts with the ability to behave sacrificially. Those who have good opinions of themselves seem more able to be sacrificial when encouraged to do so. Those with lower self-esteem seem more protective of themselves and less able to give to others. Maybe what can be seen here is a clear illustration of the second great commandment given by Jesus (Matthew 22:39) that "You shall love your neighbor as yourself." In this study, those who loved themselves more were able to show love to others more. It may also illustrate the truth of 1 John 4:19, "We love because he (God) first loved us." Those who more strongly felt high self-esteem, because they knew the love of God, were more able to love others and be self-denying. The possibilities for religious education are many.

The implications of this study are encouraging in two ways. First, they suggest that reminding persons that they should ask, "What would Jesus do?" before they act is a perfectly legitimate thing to do. God does have a will for how people behave and asking God for guidance is important. Weekly worship and daily devotions are ways to keep God's will at the forefront of people's minds. Second, this study's implications remind us of the importance of good self-concepts. More often than not, self-concepts in youth and adults are determined more by what is happening to them outside of church than within. Sensitive ministers need to keep reminding themselves of how vulnerable people are. They should attend to their parishioners' needs to be supported and encouraged. It is hard to be ethical when one's self-esteem is threatened.

Conclusion

This chapter has reviewed three studies dealing with religion and morals. As I said in the beginning, findings of these and previous research relating religious faith to ethics have provided mixed results; sometimes religion seems to evoke morality, sometimes it does not. Hopefully, reflecting on the procedures and conclusions of Hoagland's study of moral judgments and types of religiousness, Darley and Batson's study of the situational determinants of helping behavior, and Raney's study of the impact of assuming Christ's role on sacrificial behavior, have stimulated readers to think about ways to increase the likelihood that religious persons will also be ethical persons. Nevertheless, it is important that we should never forget the human tendency toward sin and the words of St. Paul, "I can will what is right, but I cannot do it. For I do not do the good I want, but the evil I do not want is what I do. . . . So then, with my mind I am a slave to the law of God, but with my flesh I am a slave to the law of sin" (Romans 7:18b–19, 25b). No amount of planning will change this human condition. Our ministries must accept this at the same time that we militate against it! On the other hand, the paradox of the gospel is that God forgives us again and again and that God's acceptance of us is not dependent on our "good works" (Ephesians 2:8–9).

For Further Reading

C. Daniel Batson and W. Larry Ventis, *The Religious Experience: A Social-Psychological Perspective* (New York: Oxford University Press, 1982).

C.E. Lenski, *The Religious Factor*, rev. ed. (Garden City, NY: Macmillan, 1963).

Chapter 5

Can Religion Make You Well?
Religion and Mental Health

The relationship between religion and mental health is a topic about which much has been written—pro and con. Early in this century, psychiatrist Sigmund Freud wrote about the deleterious effects of religion on psychological development and predicted that religion was an illusion that had no future.[1] More recently, attorney Richard Yao founded a group named "Fundamentalists Anonymous" designed to help people overcome the so-called "emotional distress" of a conservative religious upbringing. Although Yao, somewhat naively, labeled as "fundamentalist" almost all Christians who did not fully agree with his liberalism, he reflected a tendency among many to label certain types of religion as antithetical to mental health. Among this group are counselor Donald Sloat, who titled his recent book *The Dangers of Growing Up in a Christian Home*,[2] and a California clergyman named Booth, who has appeared on a number of television talk shows warning the public about the bad effects of what he has termed, "religious addiction."

While the cautions of Freud, Yao, Sloat, and Booth have been heard by many, the most vocal contender that religion is bad for mental health has been psychologist Albert Ellis, the founder of Rational Emotive Psychotherapy. Ellis, in a booklet entitled *The Case Against Religion*,[3] lists several aspects of religion which he feels keep people from becoming mentally healthy. These include his contentions that religion

—makes people feel guilty and preoccupied with repentance when they should be accepting their humanness and getting on with life;

67

—encourages people to depend on God for direction
when they should be autonomous and self-directed;
—indulges people's desire for certainty and predictability
in life when they should be willing to live courageously
with ambiguity and precariousness;
—allows people to think that change comes about by mag-
ical rituals rather than by logical reasoning and hard
work.

Nevertheless, as with several of the topics discussed in the
previous chapters, the results of controlled research on religion's relationship with mental health have not fully supported
these detractors of religion. For example, in a survey of one
year's admissions to Ellis's own counseling center in New York
City, no relationship, either positive or negative, was found between the seriousness of the problems people brought to counseling and the amount of their religious involvement.[4] Ellis'
views are well publicized and one might expect that those seeking counseling here, of all places, would reflect a strong negative relationship between **more** religiousness and **less** mental
health. This was not true. In fact, there was a slight, but not
significant, tendency toward the opposite relationship, less serious disturbance and more religiousness.

The best interpretation of these data, however, is to state
"no relationship—neither positive nor negative." If this conclusion is generalized, it would support a minority opinion that
religion and mental health are two states which are influential,
but unrelated, parts of people's lives.

The idea that religion and mental health are separate enti-
ties is confirmed in a review of all research on the topic up to
1980 by psychologist Allen Bergin.[5] Bergin concluded that the
contention that religion was more associated with emotional
disturbance and mental health was simply not supported by research. However, the reverse was not true either. The evidence
was simply inconclusive. About as many studies found religion
to be associated with mental health as with mental disturbance.
Bergin contended that the studies were hard to compare because of various differences in the ways that "religion" and

"mental health" were measured. General conclusions were difficult to draw.

As an example of the ways that results differ depending on the way in which religion and mental health are defined, Bergin, in an in-depth study of students at Brigham Young University, concluded that the mental health of those who had adhered without faltering to their family's Mormon faith was significantly higher than a group of students who had returned to Mormonism after having fallen away.[6] Scores on standardized personality inventories were used to define mental health. Religion was defined as "adherence to family religion" and mental health was defined as "scores on standardized personality tests."

Bergin's research illustrates how important it is to clearly describe what one means when one used the term "mental health" and what kind of religion is being considered in answering the question of whether religion provokes either mental health or illness. In understanding these studies or reaching conclusions, it is critical to ask: "What kind of religion is related to what kind of mental health?" Several recent studies have found that there is, indeed, a positive association between religion and mental health when these terms are defined in a definite and explicit manner.

These studies confirm, in part, what the Jewish/Christian scriptures have always promised, namely, that faith brings joy and contentment (Isaiah 26:3). Christian belief has promised abundant life here as well as eternal life hereafter (John 10:10). It should probably come as no surprise when research confirms these truths.

Although religion should not be construed as **entitling** persons to health and happiness,[7] there does seem to be a relationship that cannot be denied—at least in the investigations that we have undertaken. It seems to me that we become enmeshed in a difficult theological problem when we assert, as it has been reported that the senior pastor of the Full Gospel Church in Seoul, Korea, contends, that God intends to bless Christians in three ways—health, wealth, and happiness. I am comfortable with seeking the answer to whether religion is related to the first, happiness, because I assume happiness to be a prime aspect of mental health and I believe mature faith should have its effect on positive emotions. I shy away from the assertion that faith guarantees health and wealth because that idea seems to imply a divine favoritism with which I have continuing problems. I also find it difficult to contend that God has an obligation to bless people materially and physically when they ask for it. I guess I have read the book of Job too often to think that there is a straightforward relationship between faith and fortune. But, once again, even in seeking the relationship of religion to happiness, it is important to remember that the terms should be clearly defined and that where different definitions of religion and happiness or mental health are used, it is likely that different results will occur.

Moving from a discussion of basic assumptions to a description of our research, it is important to clarify at least three ways in which the term "mental health" can be defined. Our studies utilize these definitions. Persons can be said to be "mentally healthy" when they are (1) no longer upset, (2) functioning adequately, or (3) very, very happy. The first could be termed a **negative** definition of mental health; the second a **normal**; and the third a **positive** definition.[8] If someone declares, "I am not depressed today," they are using a negative definition. Health is defined here as the "absence of disturbance." If someone declares, "I feel good; things are going along well for me," they are using a normal definition. Health is here defined as "adjustment." If someone declares, "I've really made it; I'm extremely satisfied with my feelings and behaviors," they are using a positive definition. Health is here defined as the "achievement of a desired state of mind."

In the descriptions that follow, a **negative** definition of mental health is used in the first study, a **normal** definition in the second, and a **positive** definition in the third. Briefly stated, our conclusions were that *mature* religious faith was related to

—not needing counseling, a "negative" understanding of mental health (study 1);
—adjusting to aging, a "normal" understanding of mental health (study 2); and

—personality strengths, a "positive" understanding of mental health (study 3).

A description of each of these studies relating religion to mental health follows. While the definitions of mental health varied from study to study, religion was defined the same way in each study; i.e., through the use of the "Religious Status Inventory" or the "Religious Status Interview," both of which were described in more detail in chapter 3.

Study 1: Mature Religion and the Absence of Disturbance

Graduate student Sharon Tilley compared the overall scores on the Religious Status Interview of persons in a psychiatric hospital with persons who came to visit them.[9] Matching the groups for gender, age, and education, she found that the persons in the hospital scored lower on religious maturity than their visitors. Thus, she concluded that religion was, indeed, related to mental health. And "mental health" was defined negatively defined as the absence of an emotional disturbance grave enough to require psychiatric hospitalization.

It will be remembered that the Religious Status Interview is a one-hour-long set of interview questions designed to assess how well people are applying their Christian faith to their daily lives in such areas as their awareness of God, their sense of God's benevolence and direction, their giving and receiving forgiveness, their participation in organized religion, their experience of fellowship with other persons, their concern for ethics, and their openness to others whose faith was different from theirs. Thus, "religion," as measured in this research, was not simply adherence to a creed or attendance at religious events. The religious variable was a measure of practice and application. In terms often used today, religion was understood as "spiritual development." Those who scored highly on the Religious Status Interview were assumed to have developed spiritually beyond the surface indices of religious affiliation. In chapter 3 this measure was labeled "religious **maturity**," to indicate that it referred to a kind of religion that went beyond the average, beyond custom.

Thus, Tilley's conclusion that religion was associated with mental health, negatively defined as being less emotionally disturbed, defined religion in a specific manner. One could not conclude that religion in general or a simple "yes" answer to the question, "Are you religious?" would result in the same association.

In an extension of her earlier study, Tilley compared overall scores on the Religious Status Interview of persons undergoing **out-patient** counseling and persons not seeking counseling help. These were persons who were not hospitalized but who were distressed enough in their adjustment to seek counseling help.

Again, matching for gender, age, and education, she found that those not receiving counseling were more religiously mature than those who were. The earlier study had simply compared visitors with patients. She was interested in knowing whether the difference in religiousness she observed there would also be found when the comparison group of persons was not hospitalized.

Not only did she confirm that greater religious maturity was associated with mental health, negatively defined as not being counseled, but she also observed that the religious maturity scores of the out-patients were higher than the in-patients she had previously studied. This resulted in her proposing that greater mental health, defined negatively along a continuum from not seeking counseling at all, to being counseled, to being a patient in a psychiatric hospital, was related to a greater ability to apply the tenets of one's religious faith as seen on higher to lower overall scores on the Religious Status Interview.

Study 2: Mature Religion and Being Able to Handle Stress

In another study utilizing the Religious Status Interview, Bruce Atkinson studied how a group of Christian women were handling the stress of growing old. The women were all ambulatory residents in a retirement home and ranged in age from the mid-70s to the early 90s. Using standardized measures of anxiety, depression, and worry, Atkinson assessed how these indices of psychological distress related to religious maturity.[10]

Since all of these women had lived long enough to have experienced some, if not many, stressful events, it would be expected that they would be, quite naturally, under some duress at this time in their lives. Atkinson assumed that those who had experienced more losses, more disappointments, more tragedies, and who had less financial and family resources would report greater distress. So, he designed a questionnaire to determine the number, the kind, and the recency of such stress-filled experiences. This scale, called the Adult Life Event Checklist (ALEC) is printed in the Appendix replete with directions on how to score it. You can use it in your parish work to give you an indication of how much stress parishioners have experienced and how long ago things happened. The checklist assumes that things that happened more recently are more stressful than those which occurred long ago.

After getting scores on the ALEC, Atkinson statistically controlled for the effect of these differences to see if religious maturity would still affect how they were feeling at this time in their lives, i.e., their mental health. Mental health, in this instance, was defined "normally" in the sense of better adjustment to their life-situations. It was assumed that those women who had less worry, anxiety, and depression could be judged to be more mentally healthy even after differences in the amount and kind of stress events they had experienced in their lives were taken into account. As before, "religion" was defined as religious maturity—understood as higher scores on the Religious Status Interview, the aforementioned scale of religious maturity.

The results confirmed the prediction. Controlling for age as well as for the number, seriousness, and recency of stressful life events, those women who reported that they were experiencing less *dis*tress tended to be those with greater religious maturity. The conclusion was that their faith was functioning in their lives to provide them with less worry, anxiety, and depression quite apart from how old they were and the stressful events that they had experienced in their lives. As noted, the type of "mental health" definition being used here is termed "normal" in the sense that it refers to better adjustment to everyday experience.

Study 3: Mature Religion and Personality Strengths

In Tilley's study, mental health was defined negatively as the absence of illness. In Atkinson's study, mental health was defined normally as the ability to adjust to life with less distress. In this third study, conducted by Susan McPherson, mental health was defined **positively** as the presence of desirable personality traits.[11] These "traits" could be thought of as "personality strengths" that are some persons have developed but that others have not, such as self-esteem, ego strength, happiness, etc. When persons are found to possess these traits to a great extent, it is important to ask whether such characteristics are associated with more religious maturity. In a study of several hundred persons who had been administered the Religious Status **Inventory**, a paper-and-pencil form of the Religious Status Interview described earlier, McPherson compared personality traits in a sub-sample of persons who had the highest and the lowest overall religious maturity scores. The traits she assessed were personality strengths seen in scores on the Sixteen Personality Factors Test (16 PF), a widely used measure of personality traits standardized on the general public. She found that higher scores on religious maturity were associated with greater intelligence, more bold venturesomeness, and stronger imaginativeness. Greater religious maturity was also related to less anxiety and lower guilt proneness. These traits were seen to be personality strengths that went beyond normal adjustment and everyday functioning. Thus, McPherson concluded that religious maturity was related to mental health understood in a "positive" sense as having achieved a way of living that was above average.

Conclusions

Admittedly, these conclusions are somewhat tentative in that they are limited to specific, and somewhat unique, definitions of both religion and of mental health. However, that may just be the point at which the results should be taken most seriously. The future may be no different from the past. Surveys of religion and mental health a decade from now may be inconclusive as long as many varied definitions of mental health and religion are lumped together in the conclusions that are reached.

Most importantly, it is my firm conviction that only **mature religion**, or **optimal** religious functioning, will be found to be related to mental health, however **mental health** is defined. It is only when religion is a strong force in life or when religion is functioning in an above-the-average manner that it can be expected to play a part in good human adjustment. General religiosity, creedal assent, or church attendance will not predict mental health.

A recent rereading of John Stuart Mill's *On Liberty*[12] convinced me that this insight is not a new one. Writing over 150 years ago, he stated:

> To what an extent doctrines intrinsically fitted to make the deepest impression upon the mind may remain in it as dead beliefs, without being ever realized in the imagination, the feelings, or the understanding, is exemplified by the manner in which the majority of believers hold the doctrines of Christianity. By Christianity I here mean what is accounted such by all churches and sects—the maxims and precepts contained in the New Testament. These are considered sacred, and accepted as laws, by all professing Christians. Yet it is scarcely too much to say that not one Christian in a thousand guides, or tests his individual conduct by reference to those laws. The standard to which he [sic] does refer it, is the custom of his nation, his class, or his religious profession. He has thus, on the one hand, a collection of ethical maxims, which he believes to have been vouchsafed to him by infallible wisdom as rules for his government; and on the other a set of every-day judgments and practices, which go to a certain length with some of those maxims, not so great a length with others, stand in direct opposition to some, and are, on the whole, a compromise between the Christian creed and the interests of worldly

life. To the first of these standards he gives his homage, to the other his real allegiance.

I believe our research demonstrates this point. Human behavior is determined by a number of influences. Average religiosity impacts mental health very little, if at all. Only mature religiosity, which goes beyond what is customary, can be expected to have much influence on mental health.

Therefore, I have some confidence in the conclusions reported in this chapter because they utilize a measure of "mature" religion that is multidimensional and that presumes faith can be put into practice at an above average level in persons who are spiritually developed. Nevertheless, there is still much unfinished business to accomplish before we can make firm statements of unquestioned validity. We need to have some evidence that goes beyond simply relating self-report questionnaires to one another. Unfortunately, too many of the studies reported in this chapter are limited in this way. Perhaps the next step would be to see if greater religious maturity, such as is measured by the Religious Status Interview and Inventory, is related to judgments about mental health by other people who know participants well and actual behavior that we would all agree indicates mental healthiness.

For Further Reading

John F. Schumacher (ed.), *Religion and Mental Health* (Oxford: Oxford University Press, 1992).

H. Newton Malony (ed.), *Psychology of Religion: Personalities, Problems, Possibilities* (Grand Rapids, MI: Baker Book House, 1991).

Chapter 6

Are Sermons Better Than Sleeping Pills? The Boon and Bane of Preaching

Preaching is a topic in which all pastors will be, or should be, interested. Most homiletics classes have not included reports of the research on sermonic effectiveness. Nor have practice preaching classes considered the reports that almost two-thirds of parishioners report they go to sleep during preaching. This chapter will review studies of preaching—its intent and its effects. While it is obvious that delivering homilies or sermons is by no means all that pastors do, preaching remains a prime basis on which ministerial effectiveness is judged. Practical ways to use the research conclusions in preparing and presenting sermons will, hopefully, make this chapter a valuable one.

Interestingly enough, not one of the studies to be considered here deals with the length of the sermon. This is a serious omission. As the old maxim suggests, "The mind can absorb no more than the seat can endure." One wonders why that truth has been so long in coming to Protestant worship. It is a mystery how folk could have ever tolerated hour-long preaching or day-long meetings. The Anglican and Catholic traditions seem to have learned long ago that "shorter is sweeter." As a school-age boy, I can well remember the first time my mother played hookey from our Methodist church and took me to a nearby Episcopal service. I insisted on shaking the priest's hand and sharing, "You're the first preacher I've ever heard who didn't give me a headache." The subject of his sermon has long since faded in my memory, but the value of shortness has remained.

As a much older person, I think that what was true of me as a youth is even more true as an adult. I recall, and apply the lessons of, many sermons that were less than fifteen minutes in length, but very few that were longer. I believe that research would prove that my reactions were normal and that most persons would agree with me if they had a chance to express their opinions.

Although they only assessed retention of a short religious message, Pargament and DeRosa[1] found that only a third to a half of the content was remembered. They concluded, in support of my contention about people's preference for shortness, that "... much of the information presented in a complex lengthy religious message will not be remembered. More information may be retained from the shorter religious message in which a few points are made well."

Turning to a more detailed discussion of such studies as Pargament's and DeRosa's, this chapter will consider three research investigations and one theoretical essay. Issues that these studies have addressed include: (1) the "restricted communication" character of preaching; (2) the influence of background, beliefs, and attitudes on memory of sermons; (3) the influence of content and style on sermon impact; (4) the difficulty in training ministers to be better preachers.

Preaching as "Restricted Communication"

Communication specialist, Duane Litfin, in an article entitled "In Defense of the Sermon," compared "restricted" and "unrestricted" communication.[2] Restricted communication refers to those types of social interactions where the communication is one-way, and those receiving the message have no chance to give feedback or interact with the communicator. Unrestricted communication refers to those types of social interactions where each member of the group has the opportunity to respond and express reactions to the communicator at any time during the event.

Litfin is correct on two counts: first, his observation that the structure of worship makes sermons or homilies "restricted" communication and, second, his conclusion that the results of research on communication-in-general suggests that "unrestricted" communication results in greater accuracy, less negativity, and higher agreement. He seems to suggest that the problems with the sermon are overcome by the other opportunities people have through fellowship groups and religious education classes to interact with leaders and discuss ideas.

What Litfin seems to miss, perhaps because he comes out of a free-church tradition, is the unique "restricted" character of the sermon. He undervalues the qualitative difference that exists between sermons and other types of communication. Theologically, sermons are messages from God. They are pronouncements to be listened to—not discussed. This statement may sound presumptuous but it is not meant to be so.

The question asked by one of Philip Brooks' elderly parishioners illustrates this basic presumption about the nature of sermons. As Brooks passed by on his way into the church, the old man asked, "Have you got a fresh message from God for us today?" Worshipers do not expect to interact with ministers as they preach. They have come to listen, not give feedback. Their expectations are different than when they argue politics or listen to salesmen. Even though in the liturgy parishioners are expected to express themselves, when the time comes for the homily they prepare themselves to listen.

The essence of the sermon is supposed to be an explication of the meaning of scripture, which also is "restricted communication" in that it is considered to be the word of God and has been listened to with thanksgiving rather than feedback. Ordained clergypersons, having been approved by the church as able to exegete or exposit the truth of that scripture, speak for God. They are assumed to be channels for the divine in a manner dissimilar to politicians and salesman or, even, teachers.

The uniqueness of this assumption can be seen in the way that British common law safeguarded two types of human relationships: one vertical, and one horizontal. On the one hand, persons were entitled to a confidential horizontal relationship with someone like themselves; i.e., a friend, or counselor. On the other hand, persons were entitled to a confidential vertical relationship with the divine. Guarantee of the absolute privacy of the horizontal relationship can be seen today in the attorney-client privilege. The vertical relationship is safeguarded in the priest-penitent privilege. In the case of the priest-penitent relationship, the assumption is that the priest, or minister, represents God to the person. As it is in the confessional, so it is in the sermon. When the minister speaks, the penitent or parishioner listens. Feedback is out of the question because it is assumed that God has spoken. The communication is "restricted" and that is as it was intended to be. The sermon is a proclamation of truth, not the lifting up of items for discussion.

This is not to say, however, that ministers should pay no attention to the impact of their preaching. As will be seen in the studies to be described below, there is warrant for reflection on both style and content. In spite of the unique character of sermons, preachers still perform the task in idiosyncratic ways—as every parishioner will attest. Litfin states it pointedly: ". . . a sermon, regardless of how strongly expository, is not God's word per se. It is inevitably man's [sic] word about God's Word." The preacher is a channel for God, not God incarnate.

As Liftin's essay suggests, it is perfectly appropriate and, even obligatory, that opportunities be provided for worshipers to give feedback to their ministers about how well they have understood, remembered, and applied the sermons they have been hearing. There are many innovative ways to get this feedback, and clergy should use their creativity in designing them. At the very least, surveys, sermon feedback committees, scheduled discussion meetings, and encouragements to react and respond all should be added to the more routine shaking of the hands and expressions of appreciation given clergy at the back door of the church after worship services are over. Clergy are no more immune than all other communicators to idiosyncrasies, "hobby-horses," off-days, limited knowledge, family pressures, inadequate time to prepare, and just plain dullness. It is no secret that what is bad can get worse. It is also no secret that what is good can get better. People can change, even preachers!

Remembering Sermons as a Function of Parishioner Characteristics

Parishioners differ in beliefs, background, and attitudes. They bring themselves to worship. Considering whether and how these personal differences affect the remembrance of sermons is the topic of this discussion of Pargament's and DeRosa's study noted earlier. They designed three short religious messages and assessed how well they were remembered by college students. Although not conducted within a sermonic situation, the results of their study can be applied to actual preaching.

The religious messages were designed to represent three types of belief: (1) belief that God controlled life and that people had little power (High God-Low Personal Control); (2) belief that both individuals as well as God controlled life (High God-High Personal Control); and (3) belief that, while God created persons, they, not God, controlled their destinies (Low God-High Personal Control). Each of the statements was one paragraph in length and included both statements of beliefs and scripture passages to support the position.

Over 300 college students were assigned to listen to one of the messages in their weekly discussion groups. Several weeks prior to the experiment they used scales to measure their religiosity as well as their beliefs about how much control they or God had over their lives. After listening to the tape-recorded messages, the students were given several measures of memory: Open-ended recall, Probed recall, Fill-in-the-blank, and Multiple Choice. Their memory was then compared with their personal beliefs and background.

Several characteristics of the students were assumed to influence their memory for these religious messages. Memory has been found to be related to the ability of people to express themselves verbally, and verbal ability has been found to be a function of intelligence. This was found to be true. Scores on an intelligence test were found to be related to memory of all three religious messages.

Interest in the topic has also been found to affect memory. "Interests" determine choices—from which food people choose when they open the door of a refrigerator to which book they select at the library. In the case of these students, it is not known whether they brought their "interest in religion" with them or whether this interest was aroused by the taped messages. I am inclined to think the former is more correct. Nevertheless, scores on a test of interest were related to greater recall of all three religious messages.

"Habit" is yet another thing that seems to be related to memory. In this case the habit of greater or lesser religious activity was assessed and, as predicted, those who were more religious remembered more. This makes sense because listening to a religious message was more routine and less novel to them. They were more practiced than the other students in this activity.

More important than habit, however, is the matter of "personal beliefs." Although in the previous section, much was made of the restricted nature of sermons, communication theorists are unanimous in asserting that *every* message is filtered through grids inside the receiver before it is ever remembered, much less understood. This process is called "decoding." And one of the powerful ways in which religious messages are "decoded" is whether the message agrees with the beliefs of the listener. Beneath the central affirmation of belief in Jesus and the words of the creeds lie a myriad of personal interpretations and convictions. Personally, I am convinced that today there is probably greater diversity within the average congregation of whatever denomination than exists among the historic dogmas which have separated Christians.

In this study of college students, the contention that differences in beliefs would affect memory was borne out. On measures of "God-control" and "Personal-control," students who rated high and low on these scales remembered more of the religious communications that matched their beliefs. It seems as if people recall more of those messages that agree with beliefs they bring to the event. There was some evidence that listeners did more than just forget the messages which contradicted their beliefs. They tended to distort what they heard to fit their previously held position. Unfortunately, preachers have little knowledge of these individual differences in their parishioners. Even more important, this rule-of-thumb provides little information on how to change beliefs if the minister was convinced that those convictions were in error.

These inside-the-person variables are important. Intelligence, interests, habits, and beliefs are critical influences on how well a sermon will be remembered—if this experiment among college students illustrates a truth. I think it does. But I also think that clergy would tyrannize themselves into paralysis if they spent too much time trying to adapt their sermons to these realities. First of all, the differences are so wide and pervasive that they are impossible to measure accurately. In our culture there is no speaker who has to address an audience that differs more in so many essential ways than does the priest or minister. The age-span in the average congregation is enough by itself without considering parishioners' interests, habits, beliefs and IQs! Second, perhaps the best that can be done is to approach sermon preparation prayerfully yet humbly and confidently; prayerfully in the conviction that God does, indeed, have a message to give to the people, and humbly confident that the clergyperson can be a true channel for that message to break through all individual differences among the worshipers.

Sermon Content and Style of Presentation

Nevertheless, the frustration of all attempts to meet the individual needs of every parishioner should not be used as an excuse for preachers to spend no effort reflecting on their style of presentation or content of their sermons. Pargament and Silverman[3] undertook a study entitled "Exploring Some Correlates of Sermon Impact on Catholic Parishioners." Although they assessed some background characteristics and religious practices of the parish members they surveyed, they found that the strongest influences were due to their perceptions of the style and content of the sermons themselves.

There were seven questions which made up an "impact" scale. These were: Does the preaching of your clergy

—Help you better know Jesus Christ?
—Move you to lead a more Christian life?
—Help you to understand and respond to the Word of God in the Scriptures?
—Give you something practical for your daily life?
—Give you new food for thought and prayer?

—Move you to proclaim Christ to those who do not know
him?

—Indicate compassion and sensitivity to the needs of the
people of this parish?

Over 250 members in fifteen parishes provided answers to
these questions along a five-point scale ranging from "always"
to "never."

Overall, sermons delivered in these parishes were rated as
having a moderate impact on these parishioners (average ratings of about three). The strongest impact came from those sermons that had clear and central topics, were logically and
clearly developed, were not repetitive, were relevant to real
life, and showed that they were well prepared. A moderate relationship between a clear speaking style, natural use of ges-
tures, good eye contact, and a natural speaking pace and sermon impact was also found. Although, as noted earlier, sermons
had greater impact among those who were more religious and
better educated, the far greater influence was from the content
and style themselves.

Since the survey covered fifteen parishes, Pargament and
Silverman were interested in whether clergy in certain parishes
were having greater impact through their sermons than clergy
in other parishes. They found that this was so. Thus, the conclusions that style and content were strong determiners of sermon impact **across** parishes were tempered by the fact that in
some parishes style and content were not good. There were,
indeed, individual differences. Some priests were doing a better job than others.

Applying sermon content to the needs of individuals can be
easier said than done, as any experienced minister will agree. I
well remember the testimony of Roy A. Burkhart, well-known
pastor of First Community Church, Columbus, Ohio, during
the 1940s and 1950s. He prepared his sermons on Sunday
mornings as he reflected on his visits with church members during the week. His sermons were reflections on the needs of the
people he had counseled. The impact of his sermons was great
enough to attract huge crowds and he was judged to be one of
the nation's outstanding clergypersons. Had his church mem-

bers been a part of Pargament's and Silverman's survey, his sermons would have gotten high ratings on the questions: "Does the sermon give you something practical for your daily life? . . . give you new food for thought and prayer?"

But it should be said that Burkhart was a "free spirit." He had a reputation as a maverick who paid little regard to tradition. I would venture that he probably paid little attention to the necessity of preaching from the Bible, much less the commitment to use the Lectionary. Burkhart bypassed these constrictions and would often not mention scripture or the Christian revelation in his sermons. Most Protestant and Catholic clergy do not have this freedom, although they would probably express strong intent to make their messages relevant to life experience. The difficulty that Burkhart found in consistently relating the biblical message to the affairs of daily life is well known to the average clergyperson. Yet, as this study shows, when this is done greater sermon impact will occur.

Toward the end of their study, Pargament and Silverman discuss several implications of their study, one of which is that preachers should be trained in better communication. The final section in this chapter describes such an effort.

Training Clergy To Be More Effective Preachers

Retraining is one way to improve performance. Most seminaries have continuing education workshops on preaching. Little is known about the effectiveness of these training events. However, one such effort to measure the effect of sermonic training was noted in Burley Howe's research entitled "Defining Ministerial Effectiveness in Terms of the Change Effect on Those Ministered To."[4] Howe studied changes in sermons preached by pastors who had been trained in a model of human needs as compared to those who had not received such training.

Howe suggested that the impact of the sermon on people's lives was one of the prime indices of ministerial effectiveness. He set out to demonstrate that those sermons which more clearly addressed human needs would have a significant effect on parishioners' life-adjustment and on their ability to cope with stress. In an effort to assess this possibility, he selected four churches—two urban, two suburban—matched for size and longevity of clergy. He trained one of each type in a model of sermon impact based on preaching to meet human needs over a two-month period of weekly meetings. At the end of this training, he surveyed a sample of worshipers in each of the four churches on several Sunday mornings in an effort to assess whether they felt the sermon was relevant to their life experiences and whether they had been helped to cope with life by the sermon.

This survey of the worshipers was based on the assumption that the preaching of those ministers who had been trained would reflect what they had learned and be more relevant to human needs than the preaching of the two ministers who had not been so trained. Unfortunately, the study broke down at this juncture. When raters, who did not know which clergy were trained and which were not, attended several services in each of the four churches they were unable to make a distinction. They could not reach agreement on which sermons reflected training in the meeting of human needs more than other sermons. And, most importantly, they were unable to determine which ministers had been exposed to training and which had not.

The results of Howe's research are discouraging. In contrast to the more common short-term, continuing education training in preaching offered by seminaries, it would seem as if his weekly, two-month-long training would have been more effective, but it was not. However, we do not know what the preaching of these four pastors was like **before** the study began and that is a significant weakness of the design. It could be that they were already uniformly effective in preaching to meet the needs of their parishioners. It could also be that, quite by chance, the two clergy who were trained were much weaker in relevant preaching than the two who were not trained. In this case, the training would only bring them up to the level of those who were already proficient in human need preaching.

The only thing we know on the basis of this study is that the training did not make them excel above their counterparts. If the fault lies with the training itself, that can be improved with reflection and redesign. However, I suspect that some of the lack of effect may be due to long-standing bad habits which were resistant to training because the ratings that were done by the parishioners indicated that in no one of the churches were the sermons rated as relevant. Old habits don't die easily. While I am not entirely pessimistic about change in adult life, I do have to admit that the evidence from the psychology of learning indicates that change only comes with great effort. In most cases, it does not occur. Perhaps we should not be surprised that these results support the words of an old anonymous poem which go as follows:

> The sermon now ended, each turned and descended.
> The eels went on eeling; the peels went on peeling.
> Much delighted were they, but preferred the old way.

However, these poetic words introduce yet another issue; namely, should we expect an effect from sermons? At least one psychologist of religion, Benjamin Beit-Hallahmi,[5] suggests not. He concludes that research on the effect of worship is ill-conceived. It does not surprise him when studies of sermonic impact fail to find any effect. He feels that we have asked the wrong question when we look for changes in behavior as a result of worship. He suggests that we should judge religious worship in the same way that we make judgments about visits to art galleries or musical concerts. We never ask how art or music changed our behavior. We ask whether we appreciated the gallery or the concert. Like other aesthetic experiences, worship becomes part of the background of our consciousness. At best worship, art, and music provide perceptual foundations for our lives. They have indirect, contextual meaning. They do not result in direct, behavioral changes unless we go to more concerts or attend more art galleries. We grow in our appreciation for the arts, but we do not expect them to change our morals or make us more unselfish.

If Beit-Hallahmi is right we may need to do further reflection on the meaning of the sermon and what questions are appropriate if we want to assess sermon impact. Certainly there are strong voices, such as Immanuel Kant and William James, who would disagree with Beit-Hallahmi about what we should expect from religion. Both of these thinkers represent the long-standing biblical tradition of the writer of the book of James in contending that the ethical results or fruits of religion are of prime importance. They might assert that equating the impact of worship with aesthetic appreciation would be to miss the point entirely. Be these differences of opinion as they may, this chapter has sought to provide some food for thought about preaching that comes out of the psychological study of religion. The final answers are not yet in, nor has the ultimate research study been conducted as yet.

For Further Reading

Willard F. Jabusch, *The Person in the Pulpit: Preaching as Caring* (Nashville, TN: Abingdon Press, 1980).

David H. Read, *Preaching About the Needs of Real People* (Atlanta, GA: Westminster/John Knox, 1988).

Chapter 7

What Makes Good Clergy Good?
Being an Effective Minister

The title of this chapter, itself, implies that "goodness" and "effectiveness" are one and the same. I believe that is true; to be good as a priest is to be effective as a priest—to be good as a pastor is to be effective as a pastor.

The goodness and effectiveness of ministers are not new topics of study for psychologists of religion. Psychologists have studied religious leaders for some time. Much is known that can be applied to congregational leadership. This chapter will provide some of these findings and discuss practical ways those ideas can be used to enhance ministerial effectiveness.

Defining "Effectiveness"

The first step in this endeavor is to agree on an understanding of "effectiveness." There is a question beneath this statement, namely, "Does 'effectiveness' mean the same thing whenever, wherever, and with whomever the word is used?" or, asked in a different way, "Does being an effective **pastor** mean the same thing as being an effective **banker?**" My answer to both these questions is "No!" There is a uniqueness to parish leadership that makes "effectiveness" have a special type of meaning. "Effective" bankers and "effective" clergy may be quite different.

In my mind, being a parish priest or local minister is the most complex leadership role in our culture. No other leader is so exposed. No other leader has to speak before the membership on a weekly basis. No other leader has to deal with a membership whose ages cover the life span. No other leader's workday is so vulnerable to disruption and extension. No other leader's influence encompasses both group accomplishments and personal adjustment to the same degree. No other leader fulfills so many roles.

Even more important than all of these unique features is the fact that, in the final analysis, the goals of ministry are more spiritual than empirical; more internal than external; more motivational than factual. To think that the blackness of the bottom line on the church's financial report at the end of the year, on which bankers' effectiveness might well be judged, can be applied equally well to parish clergy is ludicrous when these special characteristics are considered. In ministry, other features must be considered. Yes, measures of clergy effectiveness go beyond a profit-and-loss statement at the close of a financial year.

At the very least, other measures have to be **added** to the income/expense report of the local congregation to truly measure the effectiveness of a local minister. At most, other measures have to be **substituted** for profit/loss ratios. The research undertaken by Laura Majovski illustrates this approach.[1]

"Hard" Measures of Effectiveness

In her effort to judge which pastors had been more effective Majovski compared the church budget, weekly attendance at worship, size of congregation, and salary in a group of seventy-one United Methodist clergy at the beginning of their ministries and five years later. The percent of change on each of these measures was labeled a "hard" indicator of effectiveness. By adding and subtracting, these measures of effectiveness could be expressed in objective numbers. They were "hard" facts.

Knowing what parish life is like, however, who of us would want to stop here and say this was all there was to effectiveness among these clergy? Knowing what roles pastors fulfill in the lives of people, many would even contend that these **hard** indicators were not even the most important reflections of effectiveness among these ministers.

"Soft" Measures of Effectiveness

Majovski agreed that hard measures could not tell the whole story of whether pastors were effective or not. In addition to these mathematically determined percentages of change, she added some parishioner-ratings of pastoral "style" and "approach." These ratings might be called "soft" indicators of effectiveness because they were dependent on subjective judgments that might differ from person to person. She had the district superintendents who supervised these pastors, the personnel committee in each church who worked with these pastors, and the pastors, themselves, rate each clergyperson on eight areas of leadership. These eight areas came out of a national study of what parishioners wanted their ministers to do, conducted by the Search Institute in Minneapolis.[2] Majovski asked raters to judge "How characteristic is this item of your minister?" on fifty-nine questions designed to evaluate whether a leader:

1—had an open, affirming style;
      —that is, the extent to which he/she related non-defensively, warmly, and supportively with parishioners;

2—evidenced congregational leadership;
      —that is, was able to inspire and unite parishioners in programs and projects that excited them;

3—cared for persons under stress;
      —that is, whether he/she was available and able to minister to people when they were facing crises in their lives;

4—undertook ministry from a personal commitment of faith;
      —that is, showed by example that his/her work was based on deep, personal convictions of the truth and power of personal faith;

5—was a theologian in life and thought;
      —that is, evidenced skill in thinking theologically

about the affairs of every day as well as about the issues of public life;

6—could develop fellowship and lead in worship;
    —that is, at one and the same time, could create a sense of unity in the congregation as well as inspire persons in worship;

7—had denominational awareness;
    —that is, could communicate effectively the meaning of their church's unique approach within the larger Christian tradition; and

8—did not possess disqualifying personal and behavioral traits.
    —that is, showed few, if any, handicapping habits that reflected on his/her modeling of the values and ethics of Christian living.

This rating scale, called the Ministerial Effectiveness Inventory, is included in the Appendix and can be used by congregations and pastors for giving feedback and self-study. As can be seen, these areas all pertain to the **way** church leaders do their jobs, their **style**. They are much "softer" and more subjective than the "hard" numbers that result from changes in size, salary, and attendance.

These softer kinds of ratings might have little to do with the effectiveness of a banker or lawyer, even if a banker or lawyer happened to be Christian. But "soft" ratings have a great deal to do with the perceptions people have of clergy and they probably outweigh the "hard" measures in importance. Although most congregations take pride in their size and their budget, when asked to rate the effectiveness of their pastors, they think more about these kinds of "soft" perceptions than about the hard facts of attendance or dollar giving. If they consider their ministers to be sincere, warm, committed, sensitive, and skilled, they will rate them as "effective" even when the congregation has lost members and the church's budget is dwindling.

These "soft" judgments of effectiveness likely override difference of opinion on major social issues. I recall a parishioner who said, "Even though I strongly disagree with my pastor on some things, I would never ask the bishop to move him to another church. The night my mother died, he was the first one to come to our home and the last one to leave. He's my pastor and I love him." This was a pastor who would probably score highly on the Ministerial Effectiveness Inventory.

"Change," The Absolute, Substantive Standard of Effectiveness

But some might comment, "Surely there are some standards other than good feelings on which to base judgments about clergy effectiveness," and this point of view should not be ignored. A study by Burley Howe,[3] entitled "Defining Ministerial Effectiveness in Terms of Change Effects in the Persons Ministered To," addressed this issue of whether there are, indeed, some absolute, more substantive standards by which to judge the effectiveness of parish priests and pastors.

Bypassing entirely hard as well as soft measures, such as described above, Howe concluded that the only true measure of effectiveness was **change** in the lives of parishioners. His study was noted in the previous chapter on preaching. It will be remembered that he trained clergy in two churches on how to preach for "life-change through faith." He taught these pastors a theory of effectiveness that emphasized people's need to grow in their ability to handle the triumphs and tragedies of life through the application of their faith. Although, as I noted earlier, he was unable to demonstrate that this training could be identified by judges who compared the sermons of trained to non-trained ministers, Howe's thesis is still a valid one.

Howe's thesis about changes brought about by effective clergy has four dimensions to it. The first, and primary, dimension of effectiveness pertains to change in **insights**. The second dimension refers to change in **understandings**. The third dimension pertains to change in **attitudes** and the fourth dimension refers to change in **actions**. Taken all together, these comprise the four dimensions of "behavior." Although behavior is

sometimes identified only with actions, insights, understandings, and attitudes are also important behaviors. In fact, actions
which can be seen are dependent on insights, understandings,
and attitudes which cannot be seen, but which are, nevertheless, very important.

The "hard" measures in Majovski's study referred only to
changes in observable actions, the fourth dimension. She measured how many attended, how much money they gave, and
how active they were in congregational programs. The "soft"
measures she studied were at the third level, subjective attitudes. Neither hard nor soft measures get at the first or second
levels, insights and understandings.

Insights and understandings are the hardest dimensions of
effectiveness to measure, but they are nearer to parishioners'
basic outlook on life. Parishioners' basic outlooks on life lie at
the core of their lives. Attitudes expressed in paper-and-pencil
questionnaires and overt acts of attendance and contributions
may not reflect how people really feel beneath the surface.
When the pressure to conform diminishes or when parishioners
are alone, what they really believe and how they truly think
may come out.

It is at this deep personal level of basic outlook, the level
of **insights** about life and their **understandings** of how faith is to
be applied to experience, that profound clergy effectiveness
lies. These were the dimensions that Howe tried to teach. He
was convinced, as I am, that true effectiveness could be seen
when levels three and four, attitudes and actions, were truly
indicative of change at levels one and two, insights and
understandings.

In a book entitled *The Psychology of Clergy*,[4] Richard Hunt
and I discussed these four dimensions of effectiveness more
fully. We were convinced that Howe was right and we sought
to explain why and how clergy could influence these changes
which indicated whether they had been effective or not. We
began by emphasizing that "behavior" was a term that should
not be limited to the fourth level, action. People are "behaving" when they gain insight, when they apply understandings,
and when they express attitudes, even though no one of these
"behaviors" can readily be seen by onlookers. In fact, as I

stated earlier, changes in these unseen behaviors are probably the more essential to true life change than more obvious behavioral acts such as attendance and participation.

Dimension 1: Change in Insight. Insights are those self-conscious awarenesses about life's meaning that come to people in worship, study, and religious experience which clergy so often plan and direct. The "born-again" reports of some Christians have gotten bad press recently, but the core idea behind these reports illustrates well the essence of the change of insight which is so central to Christian living.

At some level, for pastors to be judged effective, parishioners should point to acts of ministry in which they became consciously aware of the central truth that the meaning of their lives is encompassed by the act of God in Jesus Christ. This sounds theological, and it is, but the point is intended to be more psychological. The basic insight of the "new birth," about which Jesus spoke in John 3, is similar to that to which psychologist William James and others have referred when they speak of the new and life-changing perception that everything looks different after faith becomes real.

This core insight of faith is a revolutionary, conscious sense that is at the very center of what it means to be a Christian in word and deed. Whether this insight comes as the result of confirmation training or a Billy Graham-type decision is immaterial. I know of no clergyperson who does not desire that faith become personal at some time and in some way. When they stop and reflect on their work, most clergy consider this type of insight the basic goal of ministry. Of this I am convinced. It is the strategic starting point for the life of faith.

To have influence on life, faith has to become a conscious insight, even in those who grow up never knowing themselves as anything other than Christian. Although this change of insight is difficult to measure and may, indeed, be more gradual than immediate, it is the foundational effect that clergy should hope to induce in their members because out of this insight all other behavior flows, as the succeeding discussion will demonstrate.

Dimension 2: Change in Understandings. Understandings follow insights. Understandings flow out of insights. Understandings are dependent on insights. Understandings are the applications of insights to daily life. In the psychology of mental life, it should come as no surprise to realize that out of the basic consciousness that God has acted on our behalf in Christ, persons can "understand" the triumphs and tragedies of life through the eyes of faith. Understandings are like spectacles which parishioners put on to apply their faith to the way they interpret the events of their lives—both events that happen to them and events they cause.

Understandings refer to the developmental deepenings of faith. Whereas insight could be conceived as a "state of mind," understanding could be thought of as a "trait of perception." Whereas insights are awarenesses, understandings are applications. Increasing understanding means increasing the habit of looking at life through the eyes of faith. Some social/behavioral scientists have judged some newer religions harmful because they are totalistic, that is, they encourage people to be totally dedicated and to apply their faith to every aspect of their lives. These critics do not seem to realize that such a goal is central to older, as well newer religions. From a psychological point of view, all religious traditions, Christianity included, think that the more devotees "understand" through the truths of their faiths, the happier and more fulfilled they will be. Critics would have a difficult time proving this assumption wrong in spite of the fact that the hyper-individualism of American life covertly infers that religion should not be taken overly seriously.

Through their pastoral ministries to persons during the stages of their lives, clergy can encourage and support parishioners in the ways they incorporate faith into their subjective perceptions of the meaning of events and circumstances. Here again, the increase in understanding could be thought of as a critical measure of ministerial effectiveness that is hard to measure but central in its importance. Over time, the ministrations of parish clergy should impact the growth in faith which implies that understanding is increasing and becoming enriched. Although extremely elusive and partial, this type of change is a crucial measure of ministerial effectiveness.

Dimension 3: Change in Attitudes. This leads to the third dimension of effectiveness, a change in attitudes. If understandings flow out of insights, attitudes stem from understandings. Attitudes are feelings about, evaluations of, and inner reactions to faith interpretations, meaningful religious activities, convincing church teachings, thoughtful Christian values. Attitudes are like predispositions to respond in certain ways to opportunities to be persons of faith. They are the feelings one has when one anticipates the future. Increase in "hope," "trust," and "confidence" are good examples of changes in attitudes which indicate ministerial effectiveness.

By reflecting faithfully on the events of their lives, parishioners experience peace and joy. Following the well-known laws of learning, these good experiences leave their residue in the feelings that remain. Understandings become habits and habits become memories which leave parishioners feeling positive and enthusiastic about being religious. Ratings of approval and judgments about the functioning of pastors are the changes in attitudes that clergy evoke by their pastoral work in the events and circumstances of parishioners' lives. Effective pastoral work results in persons being favorably disposed to deeds of mercy, forgiveness, and courage.

Parishioners are always evaluating their pastors. Their evaluations and attitudes are based, in part, on their interactions with their pastors who help them apply the understanding of faith to the experiences they are having. In this work, pastoral style is as crucial as pastoral substance, as we noticed in Majovski's comparison of hard and soft measures. Attitudes are reactions to styles and responses to the way clergy play their pastoral roles. All clergy want persons to be positive in their attitudes toward being religious. Being religious involves overt action as well as inward attitudes, as will be seen in the next paragraph. Ministers are constantly hoping to change these religious attitudes from bad to good and from good to better. When parishioners are by themselves and faced with the choice of whether to resist the temptation to act as if there were no God, or whether to react faithfully in a given situation, it is their attitudes that will determine the outcome. If those parishioners point to their minister and say "He/she helped change my feelings about this or that," that will be a critical statement of effectiveness.

Dimension 4: Change in Action. The last dimension of effectiveness is change in **action**. Just as insights evoke understandings, and understandings result in attitudes, so attitudes lie at the root of actions. This does not mean that people never act in completely new ways, "out of the blue," so to speak. It does mean that on a day-to-day basis most human action results from people being drawn or repelled by their attitudes toward one kind of behavior or another. Clergy want to change overt action but they should never forget that actions have their roots in attitudes, which have their foundations in understandings, which, in turn, are based on insights.

The actions that clergy are trying to encourage are participation in opportunities to witness to, express, and apply faith to life in observable, overt behavior. This is where the program of the church becomes paramount. If clergy say they are not concerned to increase church attendance they are kidding themselves. Of course, these overt acts of attendance, participation, contribution, and witness are the hard measures with which we began this discussion. They are important and should not be discounted simply because they have their roots in more subtle human behavior. They are the final outcome of the other three dimensions (insights, understandings, attitudes) but they are the outcomes that should be encouraged and expected.

It is true, nevertheless, that behavior such as church attendance can be cultural conformity that is not based on change in insight, understanding, and attitudes. This is the insight that lies behind all of the research on Intrinsic and Extrinsic orientations to being religious. It has been presumed that overt religious action, such as church membership, could be based on a false premise which might be missed if one just noted who was and who was not at a worship service. Underneath, the motive for action might be something other than the basic insight that the most important thing that had ever happened in human history was God's mighty act in Jesus. Attendance could, possibly, be based on a desire to make customer contacts for one's business.

That is why it is never sufficient to assume that effectiveness is fully assessed when attendance and contributions are known. The real change is much deeper. Yet, as the final outcome of faith, overt, observable action is important to measure. But neither religious speech nor religious action should ever be taken as all-sufficient. As the best interpretation of the teaching of the book of James implies, faith without work is dead, but clergy should never forget that work without faith is an illusion.

It is easiest to measure action. Actions are level four. Actions are hard data. It is next easiest to measure attitudes. Attitudes are level three. Attitudes are soft data. But beneath them both lie levels one and two. Insights and understandings are the primary, and most important, changes that reflect ministerial effectiveness. And, they are very difficult to measure.

Dialogue—The Best Way To Determine Effectiveness

The only way to assess insights and understandings is to use something like the Religious Status Interview or Inventory and to discuss the results with individuals. Paper-and-pencil questionnaires can never tell the whole truth, particularly in something so much at the core of life as religious faith. In the final analysis, nothing substitutes for face-to-face dialogue.

True effectiveness in ministry can never be fully or truly measured apart from a sense of how each person is growing in and expressing his/her faith. In fact, I am convinced that the primary task of clergy is "developmental ministry," a term that refers to guidance of each individual in the insights, understandings, attitudes and actions of faithful living in a manner that results not only in passive acceptance of God's providence but active response to that love through ministry and service. The extent to which this is accomplished is the final measure of clergy effectiveness, to my way of thinking. Whatever means is used, therefore, pastors should always be on the lookout for ways to see if they are having **real** effect on the basic insight of Christian faith and the understandings, attitudes, and actions that can flow out of it.

One Other Effectiveness Consideration—Role Agreement

Up to this point, I have be addressing effectiveness as if it were mainly an individual matter. Both personal change and approval of ministerial style were focused on individuals. How-

ever, an equally important clergy task is to lead an organization, namely, the parish church. To be a minister means to be
the leader of a group. And leading means more than preaching
on Sunday mornings. Leading includes all those board meetings, committee discussions, campaign directings, staff job descriptions, assignment monitoring, and facility coordinatings
that make up a work week. And such a list does not even note
those petty, but crucial, tasks of making sure leaky roofs are
fixed, doors are locked and opened, and toilet tissue is in the
bathrooms!

I have no doubt that many readers might find the preceding discussion about effectiveness in changing individuals more
attractive than this discussion of organizational leadership. Yet
this institutional dimension of effectiveness cannot be ignored
even though not a few clergy consider the organized church a
necessary evil as the title of James Dittes perceptive book *The
Church on the Way*[5] suggests. For some church critics, the local
parish gets "in the way" of their ministry to individuals.

This negative feeling about the "organization" in institutional religion is understandable but simplistic in its awareness
of how necessary organizational life is for initiating and un-
dergirding individual behavior. Churches are necessary evils
that can become "means of grace" as the liturgy of one denomination so poignantly states. It is important for ministers to appreciate the importance of institutions and to understand how
critical is the need for them to be good leaders.

Parish clergy are, indeed, servants of the organization or
bureaucrats, in the best sense of that word. They give their lives
to institutional religion. And this is a worthy calling. Tradition
holds the role of ministers in high esteem. Their core duty is to
so lead the parish that as many persons as possible will achieve
that insight of faith which leads to the understandings, attitudes
and actions that the preceding section described. This is the
mission of the church. This is what the label "organization development" means when applied to the parish; to develop the
church as an organization so that it accomplishes its mission at
the same time that it fulfills the lives of the people involved to
the greatest degree possible.[6]

And the measure of how effective clergy are in leading is dependent on how much parishioners agree with two things: (1) what clergy do with their time, and (2) how they act when they lead. Both what they do and how they do it are aspects of **role** behavior. Although there are many effective ministers who do different things in different ways, there are few effective ministers whose parishioners disagree with what they do or how they do it, as the two studies to follow illustrate.

Sue F. Smith studied role expectations. She investigated the extent to which participation in the church was associated with agreeing with the pastor on what was most important for her/him to do. Using An Inventory of Religious Activities and Interests (IRAI)[7] she correlated a group of Protestant ministers' rankings of which roles they liked to perform with very, moderately, and inactive church members' rankings of which clergy roles they thought were more important. The assumption was that where there was greater agreement between parishioners and pastors, there would be greater participation and more involvement. Her assumption proved correct. Very active members agreed with their pastors on 80% of the rankings, moderately active members agreed 67% of the time, and inactive members agreed 38% of the time. The more they agreed with their pastors, the more active they were.

In another study Smith[8] studied a group of twelve Churches of Christ in Orange County, California, who differed greatly in their ability to gain and retain new members over the past ten years. Across all the churches she found the same results she had discovered in the earlier study—higher attendance was associated with greater agreement on which clergy roles were more important. However, the figures were not as dramatic as in the earlier study: 26% agreement among very active; 11% among moderately active, and 10% among inactive members. There did not seem to be any greater agreement on role expectations in churches which had gained and retained more members than in churches which had gained fewer new members. Thus, while these measures of overall church success did not seem to reflect greater agreement among members and ministers about what it was important for pastors to do and what they would do with their time, there did seem to be a relationship between individual participation and greater agreement on these expectations.

It is important for clergy to negotiate with their parishioners how they will spend their time. Surveys have concluded that the average clergy work week is over sixty hours. Most ministers would say that this is an underestimate and that they could do more and work longer and still not get everything done. What roles clergy emphasize and what they leave undone results from a personal decision about what it is important to do. The IRAI is a way to assess their perceived priorities. (Note 7 for this chapter indicates the way that the IRAI can be ordered.) It can be used by pastors and personnel committees to make judgments about where there is agreement and disagreement. When the results are laid out on the table, discussion and negotiation can result. Then the agreement can be communicated to the parish. Even though there are other dynamics that go into effectiveness, as can be seen in Smith's second study, agreement on role expectation will go a good distance in increasing understanding and sharing mutual expectations.

Yet another study of how agreement on role expectancies influences effectiveness was that of Susan Lichtman.[9] She surveyed eight newly-appointed United Methodist ministers on their personal preferences for **how** they would like to do their jobs. Such judgments as whether they preferred to work with groups or individuals, to make decisions alone or with committees, to delegate or supervise, to make short- or long-term plans, or to initiate plans or carry them out were assessed. At the same time, the members of the churches' personnel committees were also asked to complete the same form and indicate their preferences for how their pastors should function. Six months later she assessed the effectiveness of the ministers by having the committees complete the Ministerial Effectiveness Inventory—the same scale used by Majovski, a copy of which is in the Appendix. She concluded that the greater the agreement between ministers and their personnel committees on **how** they should function, the higher they rated the minister's effectiveness.

It is important to realize that Lichtman's research assessed agreement on "how" the pastoral role was accomplished while Smith's research assessed agreement on "what" pastors were to do. Smith measured content, Lichtman measured style. Both are important. It could be hypothesized that those ministers who agreed most with their congregations on what they were to do and how they were to do it would be those who were rated the most effective of all. This does not mean that clergy are at the mercy of whatever parishioners want. It does mean that where leaders and followers are in agreement, there will be more harmony and leaders will have more influence—in any organization, including the church. It also means that the roles and styles of ministry are always filtered through unique people and there is a need for all ministers to sit down and negotiate their duties. Furthermore, this kind of dialogue needs to be re-negotiated again and again for the most effectiveness.

Conclusion

This chapter has discussed one of the most important areas where the psychology of religion can impact church life, namely, in the area of ministerial effectiveness. Hopefully, the definitions of effectiveness and the measures for assessment will be helpful for clergy as they endeavor to do their best to present themselves to God as "workers that have no need to be ashamed" (2 Timothy 2:15). While the effect of ministry can never be totally confused with the success of banking, there are both hard and soft indications of accomplishment that do, indeed, reflect the results of ministry. However, it must be remembered that the foundational insight of God's love in Christ and understandings of life that result therefrom may be elusive and never fully known even when the parish makes marked progress in attendance and giving and even when there is strong agreement on what and how pastors are to perform. In 1829, Englishman Charles Bridges wrote a book entitled *The Christian Ministry: With an Inquiry into the Causes of Its Inefficiency*.[10] This book was reprinted in 1859. It seems that concern for ministerial functioning is no new concern. However, I would close by stating that in the novel area of parish ministry, "efficiency" and "effectiveness" may be two different things. Although I do not know the substance of Bridges' volume, I am firmly convinced that the role of ministry is so unique that effectiveness should be judged on an entirely different basis than its efficiency. I would end this chapter as I began it by reaffirming the grandeur of the pastoral role and by insisting that its effect can never be confused with banking or any other commercial venture.

For Further Reading

Joe E. Trull and James E. Carter, *Ministerial Ethics: Being a Good Minister in a Not-So-Good World.* (Nashville, TN: Broadman/Holman, 1993).

Chapter 8

Today's "Damascus Roads"—The When, Where, and How of Religious Experience

St. Paul's "Damascus road" experience has long been the norm against which all other such events have been compared. Through the centuries, Christians have reported that they, too, "met the Lord" on the Damascus roads of their lives. Only at the beginning of this century, however, did psychologists turn their attention to studying what, why, and to whom religious experiences occurred.

The first book entitled *The Psychology of Religion* was written by Edwin Starbuck[1] who conducted a massive survey of adolescent conversions which is still referred to today. His contention that conversion was a solution to the "storm and stress" of pubescence was a major theme in the pages of *The Varieties of Religious Experience*,[2] a still in-print classic in the psychology of religion written by Starbuck's teacher at Harvard, William James. Although James took note of the fact many persons were "once born" and never experienced drastic changes in their religious life, he devoted a considerable amount of space to discussing "twice born" persons—those who had experienced St. Paul-like "conversions." Conversions, therefore, are the first among four types of religious experience with which this chapter will be concerned.

Conversion Experiences

This thesis, that religious experience of the conversion type is often related to life stress, received a modern expression in the theorizing of Lofland and Stark in their essay entitled "Becoming a World Saver: A Theory of Conversion to a Deviant Perspective.''[3] Although originally written to better understand decisions to join the Unification Church, commonly known as the "Moonies," their model has been used as a general model for understanding all religious conversions.

Lofland and Stark distinguished between "predispositional" and "situational" factors in religious conversion. They suggested that these experiences occurred where persons, who were already inclined to seek religious answers to problems, were experiencing tension, stress, or dissatisfaction in their lives. These were the predisposing, "within-the-person" dynamics which increased the likelihood of conversion whenever the environment made it possible.

According to Lofland and Stark, when persons with these predisposing characteristics encounter a religious group in which a strong relationship is established with at least one committed believer and in which there is intense interpersonal interaction and only casual contact with outsiders, conversion becomes both possible and probable. These group or situational factors provide the context in which conversion often occurs.

Such predisposing and situational conditions as these would appear to still have merit in understanding, and even predicting, conversion—be it among adolescents or adults. Linking the findings at the turn of the century with this present-day model, it could be said that Starbuck identified a phenomenon which Lofland and Stark later explained. Not only does religious experience very often occur when persons are in crisis, but the availability of religious answers and the support of religious persons almost always determines whether the crisis is resolved in a religious manner.

"Conversions" are, therefore, the first type of religious experience that has been studied by psychology. Although many in mainline Protestant and Catholic churches have bemoaned the fact that some youth join new religions, such as the Hari Krishnas, or sect-like Christian groups, the sequence of events that led up to such behavior can often be understood via the Lofland and Stark model. Accusations that these nontraditional groups used coercive persuasion to enlist and maintain members is usually incorrect. There is little doubt that these groups use proven methods of influence, such as "love bombing," but, in most cases, traditional churches have only themselves to blame for not being there when youth were in crisis or providing only impersonal contact when the youth were needing close relationships. I have discussed some of these issues in an essay entitled "The Sociodynamics of Conversion."[4] In my mind there is no question but that conversions do, indeed, tend to occur where persons (1) have learned to seek religious answers, (2) are experiencing the stress of life crisis, (3) come in contact with a religious group, (4) become involved in the intense interaction and support of a religious group, and (5) are encouraged by a religious group to cut down radically the associations with other persons outside the group.

Charismatic Experiences

Turning to another type of religious experience which has been studied by psychology, at about the same time that Starbuck and James were writing, the Azusa Street revival[5] was occurring in Los Angeles. The "charismatic" experiences which typified the services during this multi-week revival illustrate the difference between those religious experiences that are "functional" and those that are "expressive."

By **functional** is meant those religious experiences, like conversions, which resolve life crises. By **expressive** is meant those religious experiences which signify that one has deepened one's relationship with God, as in charismatic experiences that reflect an indwelling of the Holy Spirit. Of course, there is a sense in which such a distinction is moot, because often what one says or does in the midst of a religious experience conveys both a solution to stress as well as a testimony to the indwelling of the divine. However, the Azusa Street revival is typically thought of as the beginning of classical Pentecostalism in America—that religious movement which has focused its worship on these kinds of religious experiences. This is a somewhat arbitrary point-in-time, however, because such "gifts of the Holy Spirit" as speaking in tongues, words of knowledge, healings and second blessings had been a part of the Holiness movement for, at least, the last quarter of the nineteenth century.

Nevertheless, these religious expressions are typically

considered to be experiences which indicate religious development in the Christian life **after** conversion. Glossolalia, or
speaking in tongues, for example, most often is considered to
reflect a deeper dedication which results from worshipers sur-
rendering their minds and their thoughts. When they speak,
the Holy Spirit of God speaks through them. As can be seen in
the Lovekin and Malony[6] study to be described below, such
religious experiences as these are intentionally sought by
Christians who want to grow more spiritual. While they are not
usually expressions which solve major problems, as in conversions, they nevertheless often result in feelings of calm, peace,
self-assurance, purpose, and hope.

In an effort to determine the personal effects of becoming
able to speak in tongues, Lovekin and Malony surveyed Christians who participated in Life in the Spirit Seminars in Episcopal and Roman Catholic churches in Southern California. All
participants indicated they were hoping to deepen their spiritual lives through participation in the Seminars. According to
the design of the Seminar, training in the charismatic gifts was
to result in the leaders laying hands on the participants at the
sixth session and, thereby, their receiving the blessing of the
Holy Spirit. Although the leaders insisted that the Holy Spirit
would be received by persons in a variety of ways, there was
high group expectation that the blessing would result in the gift
of tongues. Much of the training was explicitly directed toward
this type of religious expression.

Lovekin and Malony had these persons complete paper-
and-pencil measures of personality, of feelings, and of attitudes
prior to, during and three months after the Seminars were over.
Among the thirty-nine persons surveyed, thirteen already
spoke in tongues before the Seminars began, thirteen spoke in
tongues during the Seminar, and thirteen never became glossolalic. At neither the beginning nor at the follow-up did any of
the participants evidence psychopathology when compared to
standardized test norms of the measures.

However, the "old-tongues" group, who already spoke in
tongues before the Seminars began, were more personally and
socially integrated at the beginning than the other two groups.
The "new tongues" group showed a significant move toward

the scores of the "old tongues" group after they became glossolalic, but the "no tongues" group who never spoke in tongues showed this same tendency by the time of the follow-up testing. There were no differences among the three groups by the follow-up time. Both the "new tongues" and "no tongues" groups were as well integrated and free from hostility, depression, and anxiety as the "old tongues" group.

Thus, while the scores on the scales initially indicated that the experience of speaking in tongues had the effect of increasing mental health, the increase in personality integration among those who never spoke in tongues suggested that the supportive group experience of the Seminars itself was probably more a determining factor than the glossolalia alone. Moreover, the "no tongues" participants joined with the other groups who DID speak in tongues in rating the Seminar experience very positively and in asserting that they felt stronger than before in their spiritual lives. It is not up to psychologists to judge whether the claims that God is, indeed, speaking through the mouths of those who speak in tongues or not is true in any absolute sense. However, although psychologists do not know the language God speaks, they have found that the syntax of the speeches of those who claim to have "words of knowledge" fail to match in length or other linguistic characteristics the glossolalic utterances they claim to interpret. Furthermore, psychologists have not found any conclusive evidence that glossolalic speeches are actually existing languages that persons have never studied—in spite of the fact that this is often claimed.

Nevertheless, it should be noted that religious claims can never be proved nor disproved by scientific methods—be those claims charismatic, conversion, or mystical. Charismatic religious experiences are so unusual that they have intrigued social and behavioral scientists as well as other religious persons who have found them strange. But their differentness should not blind us to the fact that most, if not all, religious experiences make claims which lie outside the ability of science to verify.

The Lovekin and Malony study contradicts any absolute distinction between functional and expressive religious experiences. The very scales they used measured such feelings as anxiety, depression, ego-strength, and hostility. These are the kinds of feelings persons have when they are facing life crises. Changes in these feelings occurred as persons participated in Life in the Spirit Seminars designed to deepen their spiritual lives. Becoming more spiritual resulted in the increase of ego-strength and the decrease of anxiety, depression and hostility. Seemingly, religious experiences thought to be "expressive" were also "functional."

Also, this research lends support to the importance of groups in cultivating religious experiences. As in the conversion experiences discussed earlier, here the "situational" conditions highly influenced the likelihood of persons having religious experiences. All these participants voluntarily took the Life in the Spirit Seminars with the explicit intent of deepening their spiritual lives. This happened in spite of the fact that a third of the participants never became glossolalic. They still felt they had experienced the blessing of the Holy Spirit and that their lives were enriched although they did not receive the "gift" of tongues. More will be said about the critical importance of such group experiences later in this chapter. However, I would now like to discuss a third type of religious experience, the "mystical."

Mystical Religious Experience

The dictionary suggests that "mystical" experiences are those that are "beyond human understanding." Throughout Christian history, there have been reports of such events. From the time of the monastic fathers, through the long tradition of contemplative orders, to contemplative prayer in the present, Christians have contended that they, at times, have experienced awe and transcendence that went beyond their conceptual powers. In contrast to conversion and charismatic religious experiences, which are most often reported in dogmatic terms, mystical experiences retain a mysterious dimension even when worshipers perceive themselves to be in the presence of a divine person such as Christ, as opposed to "nature" experiences where the reality is much less personal.

Philosopher W.T. Stace proposed a set of five categories

for understanding mystical experience which clearly distinguishes it from those that are better described conceptually. Stace concluded that those experiences which were more "mystical" seemed to include:

—a sense of loss of self during the experience
—a profound sense that ultimate and final truth was being revealed
—a loss of words to explain fully what was happening
—strong positive feelings such as joy, ecstasy, peace
—awe and reverence in the face of profound religious mystery[7]

In less mystical experiences, according to Stace, persons did not lose a sense of their own reality, felt that what they learned was more personal and less universal, could express the experience in words, often felt anxious and depressed afterwards, and felt they could explain the event in rational or scientific terms.

As can be inferred from the above description, mystical experiences are often understood as altered states of consciousness. This is often also the experience in such charismatic events as speaking in tongues. However, here the experience is a much more active one while mystical experiences are most often experienced passively without speech.

Although there are an increasing number of persons who are seeking the quietude of mystical type experiences through retreats and spiritual direction, some social analysts have concluded that mysticism's less active, more receptive, passive stance is difficult to assume in western achievement-oriented culture which is dominated by activity and technology. In fact, one well-known psychologist of religion, Walter Houston Clark, has contended that westerners will find it almost impossible to have mystical experiences without "triggers," such as psychedelic drugs, to induce an altered state of consciousness.[8] Clark's contention has not received wide approval, but his critique of modern society may have validity in regard to the difficulty that persons will have in having mystical experiences.

Two studies exploring factors within individuals that might determine whether they had mystical experiences are Hood's[9] research on "Religious Orientation and the Experience of Transcendence" and Spradlin's[10] investigation on "The Impact of Physiological State Deviation, Mental Set, and Prior Religiosity on the Report of Religious Experience."

Hood interviewed the twenty highest scoring Intrinsic and the twenty-one highest scoring Extrinsic students from a larger sample who took Allport's Intrinsic/Extrinsic Orientation Scale, previously discussed. The majority of the students identified themselves as fundamentalist Protestants. The interviews were conducted by a person who did not know which students were Intrinsic and which were Extrinsic in their religious orientation.

It will be remembered that persons who are Intrinsically religiously oriented are thought to be those who are motivated to be religious because of the deep personal meaning it gives to their lives, while Extrinsically oriented persons tend to be those for whom religion has utilitarian value in terms of the benefits religion provides them in such areas as answers to prayers and the friendships it provides.

In the interview, students were asked to give a detailed description of the single most personal experience they had ever had. Interviewers probed their descriptions in terms of the five categories of mystical experience suggested by Stace and noted above. Judgments were then made as to whether the experience described by a given student was more or less like the transcendent mystical experience which included (1) loss of self, (2) a sense that a profound truth was communicated, (3) a difficulty in expressing the experience in words, (4) feelings of joy, peace, and ecstasy, and (5) a pervasive sense of awe, mystery, and reverence.

When their accounts were classified as transcendent or not transcendent, the Intrinsically and Extrinsically oriented students differed radically. Experience descriptions of fourteen Intrinsic students, but only three Extrinsic students, were classified as transcendent on the loss of self. The other differences were just as dramatic: seventeen to eight on truth profundity; nineteen to four on ability to communicate; nineteen to twelve on joy, peace and ecstasy; and eighteen to six on awe and reverence.

This study suggests that persons with certain types of motivations or attitudes are more likely to have certain types of religious experience. In this case, transcendent or mystical types of experience may be more typical of those for whom religion is personal, less social, and more deeply satisfying and individualistic than for those whose religion is social, utilitarian, and interactional. Another way of saying this is that we should not expect all persons to be religious in the same way.

The Spradlin study made a more general conclusion, namely, that those who have been religious in the past are more likely to have a religious experience in a strange situation than those who do not come from similar religious backgrounds. This may sound like an obvious truth but there is some warrant for not being certain whether the environment or past history would have been more likely to provoke a religious reaction. After all, some religious environments can be very overwhelming for almost anyone.

Using a scale developed to assess to what extent persons had undergone mystical types of religious experience, Spradlin had persons walk through two types of galleries in an art museum—one with religious art and one with non-religious art. He was interested in whether the gallery of religious art would provoke more of a religious experience than the secular gallery. Half the women who participated in the study were non-religious while the other half came from religious backgrounds. Before walking through the galleries, he induced in half of each group mental states of hyper-alertness and relaxed lethargy through hypnotic suggestion. He did this because previous research had found that persons were more likely to have religious experiences when their physiological states deviated from normal. As they walked through the two galleries, each woman listened to a tape recording of instructions designed to induce a mystical religious experience.

What Spradlin found was interesting. There were no differences in religious experience reported by the women who were over-excited or relaxed. Nor were any differences between the times they were in religious or secular galleries of art. However, whether one was previously religious or not did determine who reported more mystical experiences. Past religion was correlated with present experience. The women who had been religious before the study were more inclined to have mystical experiences as they walked through art galleries.

These experiences were mystical in the sense that they included loss of self, a feeling great truth was being communicated, difficulty in putting the experience into words, emotions of peace and joy, and a sense of reverence and awe. While there was no assessment of whether these women were Intrinsic or Extrinsic in their religious orientation, as was done by Hood, the same kinds of judgments about having a mystical experience were made. Past religious involvement of whatever kind influenced their expectation of and their experience under the novel condition of walking through an art gallery while listening to guided meditation.

"Traditional" Religious Experience

There is yet one other type of religious experience that should be considered. For lack of a more expressive term the label **traditional** will be used for it. This type of experience is **tradition based** in the sense that it is religious experience which occurs within the regular offices, rituals, and services of the institutional church. While many persons would not have conceived of themselves as experiencing anything unique, when prompted to focus on what happens to them time and time again as they participate in church life, they quite appropriately would label it **religious experience**. Unfortunately for the psychology of religion, too much focus has been placed on the unusual, and the routine, tradition-based experiences have been bypassed. Paul Pruyser's *A Dynamic Psychology of Religion*[11] is an exception to the rule. He spent much time in the volume detailing the penetrating way in which the sights, the sounds, the smells, and the drama of sanctuary experiences deeply affect the experience of many, if not most, church members.

I am convinced these **traditional** religious experiences are probably the norm for most Christians and that they need to be further explored both for their richness and their frequency.

Throughout the centuries worshipers have been inspired by the great music of organs and choirs. The beauty of altars and the splendor of cathedrals have filled persons with awe. Sermons have evoked insight and dedication; the elevation and reception of the host have changed lives; participation in pilgrimages and deeds of mercy have moved many to penance. One way to look at the services and practices of the Christian tradition is to say that they are all designed to evoke religious experiences that will change life. These more mundane, regular, planned, expected, and **traditional** experiences should be studied more than they have been. I am convinced that most persons are religious within the stated channels of their religious traditions than ever experience religion outside them or in exceptional ways.

Conclusions

This chapter has considered four well-known types of religious experience: the conversion or born-again, the charismatic or spiritual gift, the mystical or contemplative, and the traditional or institution-based types. British psychologist, Leslie Francis, and I are engaged in a survey that attempts to assess how common are these four types of religious experiences in comparison to one another. The checklist we are using in our study is provided below. There are thirty-six settings in which persons have religious experiences. There are nine settings for each of the four kinds of experiences we have considered. Take the checklist yourself and then use the key to see whether your religious experience is more of one type than another. Feel free to add settings that we may have missed. Use this with members of your congregation to make judgments about which type has been most common in the past for your members. Use the results to plan for settings in which different types of experiences can occur. It is important to remember that all four types have history behind them and all four have been well-respected at one time or another in the Christian tradition. In no way was the survey intended to convey a value judgment or preference for one type over another. All are valid.

INSTRUCTIONS   How important are the following experiences to your faith?
Please assess each issue by drawing a circle round one number between 1 and 5

    1 means not at all   5 means a great deal

1.	listening to the church choir	1	2	3	4	5
2.	finding God's word for me in the Bible	1	2	3	4	5
3.	experiencing something I could not put into words	1	2	3	4	5
4.	being born again	1	2	3	4	5
5.	witnessing to others about salvation	1	2	3	4	5
6.	seeing a baby baptized/christened	1	2	3	4	5
7.	feeling God's spirit within me	1	2	3	4	5
8.	feeling forgiven for sin	1	2	3	4	5
9.	receiving Holy Communion/Eucharist	1	2	3	4	5
10.	seeing the beauty of a church	1	2	3	4	5
11.	praying for others to be saved	1	2	3	4	5
12.	sensing God in the beauty of nature	1	2	3	4	5
13.	hearing the Bible read in church	1	2	3	4	5
14.	knowing I was surrounded by a presence	1	2	3	4	5
15.	attending Sunday worship at church	1	2	3	4	5
16.	attending the true church	1	2	3	4	5
17.	being prayed over	1	2	3	4	5
18.	singing gospel hymns	1	2	3	4	5
19.	feeling at one with the universe	1	2	3	4	5
20.	laying hands on someone for insight or healing	1	2	3	4	5
21.	receiving the baptism of the Holy Spirit	1	2	3	4	5
22.	being baptized	1	2	3	4	5
23.	being in a state of mystery outside my body	1	2	3	4	5
24.	feeling moved by a power beyond description	1	2	3	4	5
25.	receiving a "word of knowledge"	1	2	3	4	5
26.	praying alone in church	1	2	3	4	5
27.	attending praise and sharing meetings	1	2	3	4	5
28.	being overwhelmed with a sense of wonder	1	2	3	4	5
29.	losing a sense of time, place, and person	1	2	3	4	5
30.	hearing God speak to me	1	2	3	4	5
31.	listening to an inspiring sermon	1	2	3	4	5
32.	seeing healings happen	1	2	3	4	5
33.	singing traditional hymns	1	2	3	4	5
34.	accepting Jesus as Savior and Lord	1	2	3	4	5
35.	speaking or praying in tongues	1	2	3	4	5
36.	singing spiritual songs	1	2	3	4	5

Traditional (Institutional) 1,6,9,10,13,15,26,31,33
Mystical (Contemplative) 3,12,14,19,23,24,28,29,30
Charismatic (Spiritual Gifts) 7,17,20,21,25,27,32,35,36
Conversion (Born-Again) 2,4,5,8,11,16,18,22,34

Postword

St. Paul asks again and again in Romans, "What shall we say?" (4:1, 6:1, 7:7, 8:31, and 9:14) in response to some declaration he has made. I would ask the same of the reader, "What will you say?" in response to these descriptions of studies in the psychology of religion. Unlike the gospel to which St. Paul referred, I have no expectation that reading these chapters will transform your life. Nevertheless, I was direct in my intent that these ideas would have an effect on your ministry.

It would be perfectly appropriate for you to state your reservations. Should you say, "Most of these studies involved research on small, selected, volunteer samples; they do not exactly fit my situation," you would be correct. In almost every case, the conclusions were based on one group of people gathered together in one location. It would be proper to begin every conclusion with the qualification, "Only if these results can be generalized would it be true for me." Personally, I think most of the results are true for most parishes everywhere, but I cannot prove this. You will have to be the judge. I encourage you to not be too hasty in rejecting the possibility that the conclusions I have stated might apply to your situation.

However, I trust that knowing the limitations of these conclusions will not lead you to too quickly put aside their implications. While I recognize that most of these investigations were conducted by persons, such as myself, who do not share the responsibilities of leading a congregation, my hope is that you would at least consider the possibilities that what we have concluded could influence the way you function.

As I think about the likelihood that you will not try to apply these ideas, I am reminded of two anecdotes told by professors

117

of church administration. Both pertain to new farm agents who are trying to advise old-timers about the way they are farming. In reply to the recommendation that he allow one of his fields to remain fallow each year so that the soil could reconstitute itself, one farmer proclaimed to the new agent, "Sonny, I know what I'm doing; I ruined five farms before you were even born." In the second anecdote, a second farmer responded to the agent's recommendation that he remove a huge stone in the middle of his field rather than continue to plow around it by stating, "Young man, I can see you are not from around here. That stone is a part of that mountain over yonder; You don't move that stone."

Both of these stories reflect the grandeur and misery of being a minister. Unfortunately, many clergy are like the old farmer who resisted change. They persist in doing what they have always done in spite of the fact that their past is littered with ruined farms and churches. Habits are, indeed, hard to change. Yet, clergy should not forget that leadership is a privilege, not a right. Ingrained habits can become liabilities if they leave churches debilitated and worse off than they were before.

Nevertheless, clergy would be correct in recalling that there is a stable grandeur to the church. The church is, indeed, a rock that cannot be moved. It is an outcropping that is part of a holy mountain. Not all ideas of psychologists or farm agents are of equal value. When a farm agent suggests that a farmer move a rock which is part of a nearby mountain, the farmer may have superior insight regardless of how current the farm agent's knowledge might be in other areas. There are some aspects of the church that will not, and **should not**, change. Ministers should have the prerogative to tell psychologists what is, and what is not, negotiable.

Yet, "efficacy" and "success" should not be expletives in clergy vocabulary. Contrary to what was implied in the book title *Church Growth Is Not the Point*, church effectiveness is the point! I admit that, in the final analysis, the doctrine of the church leads us to conclude that faithfulness, rather than worldly success, is required. God has chosen the church as a means of grace and as a representative of the coming kingdom. But the church is still only the truth in an earthen vessel (2

Corinthians 4:7) and God will bring in his kingdom in spite of, as well as because of, the faithfulness of the church. Nevertheless, if the Parable of the Talents (Matthew 5:14–30) be instructive, there is an obligation for the clergy to handle wisely the responsibilities that are laid on them. They have a responsibility, at the very least, to show minimum profit on the treasure with which they have been entrusted as leaders in the church.

The old saying about "old dogs and new tricks" is discouraging, but realistic, unfortunately. Andrew Greeley in his novel *Virgin and Martyr* illustrates this prediction dramatically when he tells of the displeasure of an older diocesan priest who returns a day early from being away and finds one of the parish nuns playing the guitar in the early mass. He had not liked her style of leadership before and had, in fact, strongly discouraged her from using this type of music. Thinking he would not be back for another day, she went ahead and played the guitar as before. When he saw what she was doing, he went into a rage and interrupted her playing—right in the middle of the service. He ordered her to desist and immediately after the service phoned the bishop and demanded that she be removed. He simply was not going to change his ways to accommodate an upstart nun who thought she knew better than he did how to attract young people.

Now, not all new ideas are good ideas. There is no way to judge who was absolutely right or absolutely wrong in Greeley's story. However, there is a possibility that the old priest could have missed out on a valid improvement in the way early mass impacted young people. Being open to something novel and potentially helpful may be a trait to be encouraged.

Unfortunately, once the nun had been ordered away and reassigned, the old priest could not recall her. He missed his chance. Who knows how many times he thought back and wished he had not been so hasty in his judgments? I've had those feelings about an event that happened during the year I spent on sabbatical leave in Oxford, England. The jogging path I took led me past a bank of wild blackberry bushes. As the fruit matured, I would carry a plastic carton with me on my runs and bring back berries for my morning cereal. Needless to say, as time passed I picked the bushes clean. My hunger for black-berries did not abate, however. Only in the spring, as I was preparing to return to America, did I chance to look across the road and discover that there was a huge bank of berry bushes I had missed. It pained me to realize that they had probably been laden with blackberries which I could have picked had I bothered to look across the road. I missed my chance, however. By the time I noticed them, the berries were dried up and it was time for me to leave. I would never again be on that jogging path at blackberry-picking time. I had missed my chance. Enough said. I hope that clergy who read these chapters will not have a similar experience of realizing there were berry-laden bushes around them that they saw too late to be of use to them.

So, Paul's question still remains: What will you say to these things?

There is an English saying that I hope typifies most responses to this question. The saying is, "It was good in parts, my Lord." The saying has come to be known as "the curate's egg." It stems from the fact that curates, who are newly ordained priests, are expected to respond positively to everything presented to them by their senior vicars. In the case of "the curate's egg," the vicar cooked breakfast for his new curate. The vicar asked the curate, "How did you like the egg?" As a matter of fact, the egg was awful but respecting his duty always to respond appreciatively, the curate replied, "It was good in parts, my Lord." I would be satisfied if priests and pastors, when asked about this volume, would respond by saying, "It was good in parts, thank you." I would be even more pleased if that reply indicated that they were applying even a few of these ideas to their daily tasks!

Notes

1. Being Religious—A Psychological Point of View

1. William James, *The Varieties of Religious Experience* (New York: Mentor, 1902, 1958).

2. H. Newton Malony, "An S-O-R Model of Religious Experience," in *Advances in the Psychology of Religion*, ed. L.B. Brown (New York: Pergamon, 1985), pp.113–126.

3. G. Stanley Hall, *Jesus the Christ in the Light of Psychology* (New York: D. Appleton and Co., 1917).

4. This table is adapted from H. Newton Malony, "The Concept of Faith in Psychology," in *Handbook of Faith*, ed. J.M. Lee (Birmingham, AL: Religious Education Press, 1990), p. 81.

5. Sundén's model is discussed in Thorleif Pettersson, *The Retention of Religious Experience* (Uppsala, Sweden: University of Uppsala, 1975), pp. 39–42.

2. Boys and Girls, Black and White, Young and Old: Do People Differ in the Way They Are Religious?

1. Paul F. Barkman, "Personality Modes and Religious Experience and Behavior," in *Current Perspectives in the Psychology of Religion*, ed. H. Newton Malony (Grand Rapids, MI: Eerdmans, 1977), pp. 201–208.

2. David Elkind, "The Origins of Religion in the Child," in *Current Perspectives in the Psychology of Religion*, ed. H. Newton Malony (Grand Rapids, MI: Eerdmans, 1977), pp. 269–278.

3. Erik H. Erikson, *Identity and the Life Cycle: Selected Papers* (New York: International Universities Press, 1959).

4. Deborah Tannen, *You Just Don't Understand: Women and Men in Conversation,* (New York: Morrow, 1990).

5. Catherine S. Smith, *God-Concept, Sex-Role Perceptions and Religious Experience* (Doctoral Dissertation, Graduate School of Psychology, Graduate School of Psychology, Fuller Theological Seminary, Pasadena, CA, 1982).

6. Philip S. Pannell, *An Investigation of Religiosity: Cross-Cultural Comparisons of Black and White Religious Styles* (Doctoral Dissertation, Graduate School of Psychology, Fuller Theological Seminary, Pasadena, CA, 1987).

3. Really Believing: Is There Such a Thing as Mature Religion?

1. Gordon W. Allport, *The Individual and His Religion* (New York: Macmillan, 1950).

2. Michael J. Donahue, "Intrinsic and Extrinsic Religiousness: Review and Meta-Analysis." *Journal of Personality and Social Psychology,* 48 (1985), pp. 400–419.

3. Richard L. Gorsuch & G. Daniel Venable. "Development of an 'Age Universal' I-E Scale." *Journal for the Scientific Study of Religion,* 22 (1983), pp. 181–187.

4. Paul W. Pruyser, *The Minister as Diagnostician* (Philadelphia: The Westminster Press, 1976).

5. H. Newton Malony, "Assessing Religious Maturity," in E. Mark Stern, ed. *Psychotherapy and the Religiously Committed Patient* (New York: The Hayworth Press, 1985), pp. 25–34.

6. H. Newton Malony, "The Clinical Assessment of Optimal Religious Functioning," *Review of Religious Research* 30 (1988), pp. 3–17.

7. David L. Massey, *The Construction of the Religious Status Inventory* (Unpublished Doctoral Dissertation, Graduate School of Psychology, Fuller Theological Seminary, Pasadena, CA, 1988).

Mark Hadlock, *The Cross-Validation of the Religious Status Inventory* (Unpublished Doctoral Dissertation, Graduate School of Psychology, Fuller Theological Seminary, Pasadena, CA, 1988).

8. James W. Fowler, *Stages of Faith: The Psychology of Hu-*

man Development and the Quest for Meaning (San Francisco: Harper and Row, 1981).

4. Religion and Morals: Does Faith Make Better Persons?

1. Bernard Spilka, Ralph W. Hood, Jr., and Richard L. Gorsuch, *The Psychology of Religion: An Empirical Approach* (Englewood Cliffs, NJ: Prentice-Hall, Inc., 1985), pp. 279–280.
2. Donald D. Hoagland, *Moral Judgment and Religious Belief: An Investigation of the "Moral Majority"* (Doctoral Dissertation, Graduate School of Psychology, Fuller Theological Seminary, Pasadena, CA, 1984).
3. Julian N. Hartt, *A Christian Critique of American Culture* (New York: Harper and Row, 1967), pp. 74, 69.
4. John M. Darley and C. Daniel Batson, " 'From Jerusalem to Jericho': A Study of Situational and Dispositional Variables in Helping Behavior," *Journal of Personality and Social Psychology*, 27 (1) (1973), pp. 100–108.
5. Richard W. Raney, *Health versus Holiness: Self-Esteem, Self-Sacrifice and Perception of Christ's Ethics (Christ-Concept)* (Doctoral Dissertation, Graduate School of Psychology, Fuller Theological Seminary, Pasadena, CA, 1984).

5. Can Religion Make You Well? Religion and Mental Health

1. Sigmund Freud, *The Future of an Illusion* (Garden City, NY: Doubleday, 1927, 1964).
2. Donald E. Sloat, *The Dangers of Growing Up in a Christian Home* (Nashville, TN: Thomas Nelson, 1986).
3. Albert Ellis, *The Case against Religion: A Psychotherapist's View* (New York: Institute for Rational Living, 1971).
4. Paul W. Sharkey and H. Newton Malony, "Religiosity and Emotional Disturbance: A Test of Ellis's Thesis in His Own Counseling Center," *Psychotherapy*, 23 (1986): 640–641.
5. Allen E. Bergin, "Religiosity and Mental Health: A Critical Re-Evaluation and Meta-Analysis," *Professional Psychology: Research and Practice* 14 (1983): 170–184.
6. Allen E. Bergin, Randy A. Stinchfield, Thomas A. Gaskin, Kevin S. Masters, and Clyde E. Sullivan, "Religious Life-

Styles and Mental Health: An exploratory study," *Journal of Counseling Psychology* 35 (1988): 91–98.

7. Frederic C. Craigie, Jr., and Siang-Yang Tan, "Entitlement," *Journal of Psychology and Theology* 8 (1989): 57–68.

8. H. Newton Malony. *Wholeness and Holiness: Readings in the Psychotheology of Mental Health.* (Grand Rapids, MI.: Baker Book House, 1983): 15–20.

9. Sharon B. Tilley, *Religious Maturity and Mental Health: Verification of the Religious Status Interview* (Doctoral Dissertation, Graduate School of Psychology, Fuller Theological Seminary, Pasadena, CA, 1985). Discussed in H. Newton Malony, "The Clinical Assessment of Optimal Religious Functioning," *Review of Religious Research* 30 (1988): 12.

10. Bruce E. Atkinson, *Religious Maturity and Psychological Distress among Older Christian Women* (Unpublished Doctoral Dissertation, Fuller Theological Seminary, Pasadena, CA, 1986). Discussed in H. Newton Malony, "The Clinical Assessment of Optimal Religious Functioning," *Review of Religious Research*, 30 (1988): 13.

11. Susan E. McPherson, *The Relationship between Religious Maturity and Personality Traits: A Validity Study of the Religious Status Interview* (Master's Thesis, Fuller Theological Seminary, Pasadena, CA, 1987). Discussed in H. Newton Malony, "The Clinical Assessment of Optimal Religious Functioning, "*Review of Religious Research* 30 (1988): 13–14.

12. David Spitz, editor, *On Liberty—John Stuart Mill* (New York: W.W. Norton, 1975), p. 40.

6. Are Sermons Better Than Sleeping Pills?
The Boon and Bane of Preaching

1. Kenneth I. Pargament, and Donald V. DeRosa, "What Was That Sermon About? Predicting Memory for Religious Messages from Cognitive Psychology Theory," *Journal for the Scientific Study of Religion*, 24 (1985): 180–193.

2. A. Duane Litfin, "In Defense of the Sermon: A Communicational Approach," *Journal of Psychology and Theology* 74 (1974): 36–43.

3. Kenneth I. Pargament and William H. Silverman, "Ex-

ploring Some Correlates of Sermon Impact on Catholic Parishioners," *Review of Religious Research* 24 (1982): 33–39.

4. Burley Howe, *Defining Ministerial Effectiveness in Terms of the Change Effect on Persons Ministered To* (Unpublished Doctoral Dissertation, Graduate School of Psychology, Fuller Theological Seminary, Pasadena, CA, 1980).

5. Benjamin Beit-Hallahmi, "Religion as Art and Identity," *Religion*, 16 (1986): 1–17.

7. What Makes Good Clergy Good?
Being an Effective Minister

1. Laura F. Majovski and H. Newton Malony, "The Role of Psychological Assessment in Predicting Ministerial Effectiveness." *Review of Religious Research*, 28 (1986), pp. 29–39.

2. David S. Schuller, Merton P. Strommen, and Milo L. Brekke, *Readiness for Ministry: Volume 1—Criteria* (New York: Harper and Row, 1975).

3. Burley R. Howe, *Defining Ministerial Effectiveness in Terms of the Change Effects in Persons Ministered To* (Unpublished Doctoral Dissertation, Fuller Theological Seminary, Pasadena, CA, 1980).

4. H. Newton Malony and Richard A. Hunt, *The Psychology of Clergy* (Harrisburg, PA: Morehouse Publishing, 1991).

5. James E. Dittes, *The Church in the Way* (New York: Scribners, 1967).

6. H. Newton Malony, *Church Organization Development: Perspectives and Processes* (Pasadena, CA: Integration Press, 1986).

7. Sam C. Webb, *An Inventory of Religious Activities and Interests* (Princeton, NJ: Educational Testing Service, 1967). The IRAI is now available through *Ministry Inventories*, 180 North Oakland Avenue, Pasadena, CA 91101.

8. Sue F. Smith, *Member Recruitment-Involvement in Voluntary Organizations as Function of Leadership Role Expectations* (Unpublished Doctoral Dissertation, Fuller Theological Seminary, Pasadena, CA, 1977).

9. Susan L. Lichtman, *Ministerial Effectiveness as a Function of Job Expectancies and Personal Preferences* (Unpublished

Doctoral Dissertation, Fuller Theological Seminary, Pasadena, CA, 1989).

10. C. Bridges, *The Christian Ministry: With an Inquiry into the Causes of Its Inefficiency* (New York: Robert Cartere) (First London publication 1829, reprinted 1859).

8. Today's "Damascus Road"—The When, Where, and How of Religious Experience

1. Edwin Starbuck, *The Psychology of Religion* (New York: Charles Scribner's Sons, 1899).

2. William James, *The Varieties of Religious Experience* (New York: Longmans, 1902).

3. John Lofland and Rodney Stark, "Becoming a World Saver: A Theory of Conversion to a Deviant Perspective," *American Sociological Review* 30 (1965): 862–874.

4. H. Newton Malony, "The Sociodynamics of Conversion," in *Psychology of Religion: Personalities, Problems, Possibilities.* ed. H. Newton Malony (Grand Rapids, MI: Baker Book House, 1991), pp. 197–204.

5. Victor Synan, *The Holiness-Pentecostal Movement in the United States* (Grand Rapids, MI: Eerdmans, 1971).

6. Adams A. Lovekin and H. Newton Malony, "Religious Glossolalia: A Longitudinal Study of Personality Changes," *Journal for the Scientific Study of Religion* 16 (1977), pp. 383–393.

7. William T. Stace, *Mysticism and Philosophy* (Philadelphia: Lippincott; London: Macmillan, 1961).

8. Walter Houston Clark, *Chemical Ecstasy* (New York: Sheed and Ward, 1969).

9. Ralph W. Hood, Jr., "Religious Orientation and the Experience of Transcendence," *Journal for the Scientific Study of Religion*, 12 (1975): 441–448.

10. William T. Spradlin, "The Impact of Physiological State Deviation, Mental Set, and Prior Religiosity on the Report of Religious Experience," (Doctoral Dissertation, Fuller Theological Seminary, Pasadena, CA, 1985).

11. Paul W. Pruyser, *A Dynamic Psychology of Religion* (Philadelphia: Westminster Press, 1968).

King and Hunt Scales

The Items

I. *Creedal Assent* (.84; .83)
I believe in God as a Heavenly Father who watches over me and to whom I am accountable.
I believe that the Word of God is revealed in the Scriptures.
I believe that Christ is a living reality.
I believe that God revealed Himself to man in Jesus Christ.
I believe in salvation as release from sin and freedom for new life with God.
I believe in eternal life.
I believe honestly and wholeheartedly in the doctrines and teachings of the Church.

II. *Devotionalism* (.84; .85)
How often do you pray privately in places other than at church?
How often do you ask God to forgive your sin?
When you have decisions to make in your everyday life, how often do you try to find out what God wants you to do?
Private prayer is one of the most important and satisfying aspects of my religious experience.
I frequently feel very close to God in prayer, during public worship, or at important moments in my daily life.

III. *Church Attendance* (.82; .82)
If not prevented by unavoidable circumstances, I attend church: (More than once a week—Twice a year or less)
During the last year, how many Sundays per month on the average have you gone to a worship service? (None/Three or more)

How often have you taken Holy Communion (The Lord's Supper, the Eucharist) during the past year?

IV. *Organizational Activity* (.81; .83)
How would you rate your activity in your congregation? (Very active—Inactive)
How often do you spend evenings at church meetings or in church work?
Church activities (meetings, committee work, etc.) are a major source of satisfaction in my life.
List the church offices, committees, or jobs of any kind in which you served during the past twelve months (Coded: None—Four or more)
I keep pretty well informed about my congregation and have some influence on its decisions.
I enjoy working in the activities of the Church.

V. *Financial Support* (.73; .73)
Last year, approximately what per cent of your income was contributed to the Church? (1% or less—10% or more)
During the last year, how often have you made contributions to the Church IN ADDITION TO the general budget and Sunday School? (Regularly—Never)
During the last year, what was the average MONTHLY contribution of your family to your local congregation? (Under $5—$50 or more)
In proportion to your income, do you consider that your contributions to the Church are: (Generous—Small)
I make financial contributions to the Church: (In regular, planned amounts—Seldom or never)

VI. *Religious Despair* (.79; .77)
My personal existence often seems meaningless and without purpose.
My life is often empty, filled with despair.
I have about given up trying to understand "worship" or get much out of it.
I often wish I had never been born.

I find myself believing in God some of the time, but not at other times.
Most of the time my life seems to be out of my control.
The Communion Service (Lord's Supper, Eucharist) often has little meaning to me.

VII. *Orientation to Growth and Striving* (.79; .81)
How often do you read the Bible?
How often do you read literature about your faith (or church)? (Frequently—Never) [A-F]
The amount of time I spend trying to grow in understanding of my faith is: (Very much—Little or none)
When you have decisions to make in your everyday life, how often do you try to find out what God wants you to do? (II)
I try hard to grow in understanding of what it means to live as a child of God.
I try hard to carry my religion over into all my other dealings in life. [A-F]

Composite Religious Scales

A. *Salience: Behavior* (.80; .83)
How often in the past year have you shared with another church member the problems and joys of trying to live a life of faith in God?
How often do you talk about religion with your friends, neighbors, or fellow workers?
How often have you personally tried to convert someone to faith in God?
How often do you read the Bible? (VII)
When faced with decisions regarding social problems how often do you seek guidance from statements and publications provided by the Church?
How often do you talk with the pastor (or other official) about some part of the worship service: for example, the sermon, scripture, choice of hymns, etc?
During the last year, how often have you visited someone in need, besides your own relatives?

B. *Salience: Cognition* (.84; .81)

Religion is especially important to me because it answers many questions about the meaning of life. [A-F]

I try hard to grow in understanding of what it means to live as a child of God. (VII)

My religious beliefs are what really lie behind my whole approach to life. [A-F]

I frequently feel very close to God in prayer, during public worship, or at important moments in my daily life. (II)

I often experience the joy and peace which come from knowing I am a forgiven sinner.

When you have decisions to make in your everyday life, how often do you try to find out what God wants you to do? (VI, VII)

I believe in God as a Heavenly Father who watches over me and to whom I am accountable. (I)

I try hard to carry my religion over into all my other dealings in life. [A-F] (VII)

C. *The Active Regulars* (.86; .84)

(In 1968, called Index of Attendance and Giving)

If not prevented by unavoidable circumstances, I attend church: (More than once a week—Twice a year or less). (III)

How would you rate your activity in your congregation? (Very active—Inactive) (VI)

How often have you taken Holy Communion (The Lord's Supper, The Eucharist) during the past year? (III)

During the last year, how many Sundays per month on the average have you gone to a worship service? (None—Three or more) (III)

How often do you spend evenings at church meetings or in church work? (IV)

Church activities (meetings, committee work, etc.) are a major source of satisfaction in my life. (IV)

During the last year, how often have you made contributions to the Church IN ADDITION TO the general budget and Sunday School? (Regularly—Never) (V)

I make financial contributions to the Church: (In regular, planned amounts—Seldom or never) (V)

Last year, approximately what percent of your income was contributed to the Church? (1% or less—10% or more) (V)
During the last year, what was the average MONTHLY contribution of your family to your local congregation? (Under $5—$50 or more) (V)

Cognitive Style Variables

A. *Intolerance of Ambiguity* (.82; .82)
(Martin and Westie items)
You can classify almost all people as either honest or crooked.
There are two kinds of women: the pure and the bad.
There are two kinds of people in the world: the weak and the strong.
A person is either a 100% American or he isn't.
A person either knows the answer to a question or he doesn't.
There is only one right way to do anything.
It doesn't take very long to find out if you can trust a person.

B. *Purpose in Life: Positive* (.74; .78)
(Items adapted from Crumbaugh and Maholick)
Facing my daily tasks is usually a source of pleasure and satisfaction to me.
My life is full of joy and satisfaction.
I have discovered satisfying goals and a clear purpose in life.
I usually find life new and exciting.
If I should die today, I would feel that my life has been worthwhile.

C. *Purpose in Life: Negative* (.78; .73)
(Items adapted from Crumbaugh and Maholick)
My life is often empty, filled with despair. (VI)
My personal existence often seems meaningless and without purpose. (VI)
I often wish I had never been born. (VI)
Most of the time my life seems to be out of my control. (VI)

Appendix II

The Age Universal I (Intrinsic)–E (Extrinsic) Scale[1]

1. I enjoy reading about my religion.

2. I go to church because it helps me to make friends.

3. It doesn't much matter what I believe so long as I am good.

4. Sometimes I have to ignore my religious beliefs because of what people might think of me.

5. It is important to me to spend time in private thought and prayer.

6. I would prefer to go to church:
   (1) a few times a year or less
   (2) once every month or two
   (3) two or three times a month
   (4) about once a week
   (5) more than once a week

7. I have often had a strong sense of God's presence.

8. I pray mainly to gain relief and protection.

---

[1] Richard L. Gorsuch and G. Daniel Venable. ''Development of an 'Age Universal' I-E Scale,'' *Journal for the Scientific Study of Religion*, 22 1983, pp. 181–187.

9. I try hard to live all my life according to my religious beliefs.

10. What religion offers me most is comfort in times of trouble and sorrow.

11. My religion is important because it answers many questions about the meaning of life.

12. I would rather join a Bible study group than a church social group.

13. Prayer is for peace and happiness.

14. Although I am religious, I don't let it affect my daily life.

15. I go to church mostly to spend time with my friends.

16. My whole approach to life is based on my religion.

17. I go to church mainly because I enjoy seeing people I know there.

18. I pray mainly because I have been taught to pray.

19. Prayers I say when I'm alone are as important to me as those I say in church.

20. Although I believe in my religion, many other things are more important in life.

Key:
"I" items = 1, 5, 6, 7, 9, 11, 12, 16, 19
"E" items = 2, 3, 4, 8, 10, 13, 14, 15, 17, 18, 20

All items are scored 1–5
Possible range I = 9–45, E = 11–55

Religious Status Interview

Interviewer: _____   Interviewee: _____
Setting: _____   Date: _____

Directions for Interviewer:
1. Ask the interviewee the questions numbered 1 through 33 in order.
2. Take down his/her answers in the appropriate places in abbreviated form.
3. Score each subscale as you go along by glancing over the ratings from 1 to 7 (and sometimes back to 1 again), and *circling the one rating* which is best reflected in the interviewee's answer. Remember that a rating of 7 always reflects the most mature answer and a rating of 1 the least mature answer.
4. Do *not* ask additional questions which are not indicated on this interview. However, several prompting questions may on occasion be appropriate when the information received in the answer is not sufficient to render a rating. These prompting questions are limited to the following:
   "Could you tell me more about that?"
   "Could you explain that more fully?"
   "Can you give me an example of that?"
   "Can you think of another example?"
5. Place ratings in the blanks indicated below. Total scores within each subscale first, and then total these for an overall score. Norms have not yet been established, but the higher the score, the more mature the faith.

Scoring Totals:	A	B	C	D	E	Total
I. Awareness of God	___ +	___ +	___ +	___ +	___ =	___
II. Acceptance of God's grace and steadfast love	___ +	___ +	___ +	___		= ___
III. Being repentant and responsible	___ +	___ +	___ +	___ +	___ =	___
IV. Knowing God's leadership and direction	___ +	___ +	___			= ___
V. Involvement in organized religion	___ +	___ +	___ +	___		= ___
VI. Experiencing fellowship	___ +	___ +	___			= ___
VII. Being ethical	___ +	___ +	___ +	___		= ___
VIII. Affirming openness in faith	___ +	___ +	___ +	___		= ___

TOTAL SCORE: _____

Religious Status Interview

I. Awareness of God

QUESTION: ANSWER:
1. Who or what is
   God to you?

SUBSCALE: A. Attitude toward God
RATING:
1 = This person demonstrates an indifferent or impersonal
    attitude toward God.
2 = an answer judged to be between 1 and 3.
3 = This person merely acknowledges that God has a role in
    his/her life.
4 = an answer judged to be between 3 and 5.
5 = This person stands in awe before God as a creature aware
    of his/her Creator.

QUESTION: ANSWER:
2. Who or what is
   Jesus Christ to you?

SUBSCALE:
RATING:
1 = This person has an indifferent or impersonal attitude
    toward Christ.
2 = an answer judged to be between 1 and 3.
3 = This person merely names one or two roles Christ plays in
    general but is unable to apply them personally.

4 = an answer judged to be between 3 and 5.

5 = This person mentions several of the roles Christ plays in human life and is able to apply them personally.

QUESTION: ANSWER:

3. In your *day to day*
   life, for which things
   do you depend upon
   God and for which things
   do you not?

SUBSCALE: B. Sense of Dependence on God
RATING:

1 = This person is totally independent of God. He/she completely denies God's capacity to influence their life.

2 = an answer judged to be between 1 and 3.

3 = This person overemphasizes his/her *independence* from God.

4 = an answer judged to be between 3 and 5.

5 = This person expresses awareness of his/her dependence upon the Creator, but also recognizes his/her own capabilities.

4 = an answer judged to be between 3 and 5.

3 = This person overemphasizes his/her dependence on God.

2 = an answer judged to be between 1 and 3.

1 = This person is overly dependent on God, totally denying his/her own capabilities or power to act.

QUESTION: ANSWER:

4. When problems
   seem out of
   your control,
   what do you do?

SUBSCALE: C. Sense of Creatureliness
RATING:

1 = This person shows an attitude of total resignation, giving up on life and discounts his/her own power.

2 = an answer judged to be between 1 and 3.
3 = This person is troubled by his/her creaturely limitations.
4 = an answer judged to be between 3 and 5.
5 = This person shows humility in the face of life's besetting problems and a realistic awareness of his/her own creaturely limitations but does not deny his/her own capacity for productive action.
4 = an answer judged to be between 3 and 5.
3 = This person minimizes some of the real limitations of his/her creatureliness.
2 = an answer judged to be between 1 and 3.
1 = This person is thoroughly self-aggrandizing, denying his/her own creaturely limitations.

QUESTION: ANSWER:
5. Why do you
   worship God?

SUBSCALE: D. Use of Worship
RATING:
1 = This person sees worship as something he/she *should* do as a duty or obligation.
2 = an answer judged to be between 1 and 3.
3 = This person's worship serves as a means of meeting his/her own needs.
4 = an answer judged to be between 3 and 5.
5 = This person's worship serves primarily as an expression of reverence and love toward God.

QUESTION: ANSWER:
6. In what
   situations do you
   pray to God and why?

SUBSCALE: E. Use of Prayer
RATING:
1 = This person sees prayer as something he/she *should* do as a duty or obligation.

2 = an answer judged to be between 1 and 3.

3 = This person's prayer serves as a means of meeting his/her own needs.

4 = an answer judged to be between 3 and 5.

5 = This person's prayer serves basically as a means of spiritual sustenance and communion with God, including honest expression of concerns.

II. Acceptance of God's Grace and Steadfast Love

QUESTION: ANSWER:

7. How does God seem to respond to you when you sin?

SUBSCALE: A. View of God's Love

RATING:

1 = This person views God as basically punitive, judgmental and distant, not loving.

2 = an answer judged to be between 1 and 3.

3 = This person sees God's love as conditional, as dependent on his/her actions.

4 = an answer judged to be between 3 and 5.

5 = This person views God as loving him/her unconditionally.

QUESTION: ANSWER:

8. How do *you* respond to God's love and forgiveness?

SUBSCALE: B. Response to God's Love

RATING:

1 = This person completely fails to use God's love and forgiveness as a motivation for responsible change or action.

2 = an answer judged to be between 1 and 3.

3 = This person uses God's love and forgiveness as an impetus for some minimal change.

4 = an answer judged to be between 3 and 5.

5 = This person uses God's love and forgiveness as an impetus for new living and responsible action.

QUESTION: ANSWER:

9. What feelings come
    up when you think
    of God's love?

SUBSCALE: C. Appreciation of God's Love
RATING:

1 = This person does not appreciate and experience God's love.

2 = an answer judged to be between 1 and 3.

3 = This person has some appreciation or experience of God's love, but lacks a sense of joy and gratitude.

4 = an answer judged to be between 3 and 5.

5 = This person appreciates and experiences God's love, manifested by a sense of joy and gratitude.

QUESTION: ANSWER:

10. Why do you think
     God allows personal
     suffering in your
     life?

SUBSCALE: D. Personal Meaning in Life's Problems
RATING:

1 = This person completely denies his/her problems and sorrows.

2 = an answer judged to be between 1 and 3.

3 = This person admits he/she has problems or sorrows but sees no higher meaning to them.

4 = an answer judged to be between 3 and 5.

5 = This person has the ability to find meaning in the suffering and difficulties of life. This meaning is based on trust in God and his goodness.

4 = an answer judged to be between 3 and 5.

3 = This person struggles with why God allows suffering in his/her life.

2 = an answer judged to be between 1 and 3.

1 = This person is totally unable to meaningfully integrate life's difficulties and sorrows with his/her faith.

III. Being Repentant and Responsible

QUESTION: ANSWER:

11. In general, who or
what causes your
problems?

SUBSCALE: A. Locus of Control

RATING:

1 = This person projects sole responsibility for personal difficulties or sin onto God, parents, friends, or situations.

2 = an answer judged to be between 1 and 3.

3 = This person lays excessive blame on others for difficulties or sin.

4 = an answer judged to be between 3 and 5.

5 = This person accurately perceives personal responsibility without denying other factors such as the environment in personal difficulties or sin.

4 = an answer judged to be between 3 and 5.

3 = This person tends to internalize excessive personal responsibility for difficulties or sin.

2 = an answer judged to be between 1 and 3.

1 = This person sees himself/herself as having total responsibility for personal difficulties or sin, completely denying any environmental factors.

QUESTION: ANSWER:

12. How do you handle
your own angry
feelings?

SUBSCALE: B.. Acceptance of Feelings
RATING:
1 = This person denies his/her feelings and impulses. He/she does not see them as part of being human.
2 = an answer judged to be between 1 and 3.
3 = This person is aware of his/her negative feelings, but does not accept them as a legitimate part of being human.
4 = an answer judged to be between 3 and 5.
5 = This person is aware of his/her negative feelings and accepts them as a legitimate part of being human.

QUESTION:	ANSWER:
13. How do you *feel* when you have wronged someone?	

SUBSCALE: C. Motivation and Repentance
RATING:
1 = This person's attitude of repentance is based on guilt feelings or self-depreciation rather than concern for the offended person or solution of the problem.
2 = an answer judged to be between 1 and 3.
3 = This person's attitude of repentance shows elements of both guilt and concern for the other.
4 = an answer judged to be between 3 and 5.
5 = This person's attitude of repentance is based on concern to correct the situation, a feeling of constructive sorrow.
4 = an answer judged to be between 3 and 5.
3 = This person recognizes minimal need for repentance.
2 = an answer judged to be between 1 and 3.
1 = This person completely denies any need for repentance, showing no concern for the offended person or solution of the problem.

QUESTION:	ANSWER:
14. What do you do when you have wronged someone?	

SUBSCALE: D. Requesting Forgiveness
RATING:

1 = This person completely denies or rationalizes any need to ask for forgiveness from another person.

2 = an answer judged to be between 1 and 3.

3 = This person seldom asks for forgiveness.

4 = an answer judged to be between 3 and 5.

5 = This person is able to request and accept forgiveness from others without feeling threatened or self-depreciating.

4 = an answer judged to be between 3 and 5.

3 = This person has some difficulty accepting forgiveness from others.

2 = an answer judged to be between 1 and 3.

1 = This person may ask for forgiveness, but is unable to really accept it. This individual feels very unworthy of receiving forgiveness.

QUESTION: ANSWER:

15. When someone
    has wronged you,
    how do you respond to
    him or her?

SUBSCALE: E. Granting Forgiveness
RATING:

1 = This person cannot forgive others. This individual continues to feel anger, resentment, bitterness or suspicion toward them.

2 = an answer judged to be between 1 and 3.

3 = This person forgives superficially, but still feels resentment.

4 = an answer judged to be between 3 and 5.

5 = This person is forgiving of others without experiencing continued resentment toward them.

IV. Knowing God' Leadership and Direction

QUESTION: ANSWER:
16. How do you make
    major decisions
    in your life?

SUBSCALE: A. Trust in God's Leadership
RATING:
1 = This person totally lacks trust in God's leadership, taking
    on complete responsibility for directing his/her life.
2 = an answer judged to be between 1 and 3.
3 = This person minimizes the role of God's leadership in his/
    her decision making process.
4 = an answer judged to be between 3 and 5.
5 = This person expresses trust in God' leadership for his/her
    life yet also recognizes his/her role in that process.
4 = an answer judged to be between 3 and 5.
3 = This person tends to overspiritualize guidance in life, min-
    imizing his/her own power.
2 = an answer judged to be between 1 and 3.
1 = This person demonstrates a naive trust in God, completely
    denying his/her own power to direct his/her life.

QUESTION: ANSWER:
17. What do you think
    your future is
    going to be like?

SUBSCALE: B. Sense of Hope
RATING:
1 = This person feels hopeless. He/she has an attitude of resig-
    nation in life.
2 = an answer judged to be between 1 and 3.
3 = This person feels somewhat pessimistic.

4 = an answer judged to be between 3 and 5.

5 = This person expresses an optimistic, but realistic hope based on trust in God, without denying present problems. This person is confident that God is in control.

4 = an answer judged to be between 3 and 5.

3 = This person feels somewhat unrealistically optimistic.

2 = an answer judged to be between 1 and 3.

1 = This person completely denies his/her problems, expressing a naive, unrealistic optimism.

QUESTION:	ANSWER:
18. How does your faith relate to your various roles in your family, occupation, and community?	

SUBSCALE: C. Role Identity
RATING:

1 = This person has a thoroughly diffuse or unclear role identity, which does not provide any meaning in relation to his/her faith.

2 = an answer judged to be between 1 and 3.

3 = This person has a partially defined role identity, but does not relate it to his/her faith.

4 = an answer judged to be between 3 and 5.

5 = This person has a sense of positive role identity which provides meaning in relation to his/her faith.

V. Involvement in Organized Religion

QUESTION:	ANSWER:
19. How often do you attend the activities of your church or religious community?	

SUBSCALE: A. Level of Involvement
RATING:
1 = This person attends church only on holidays.
2 = This person attends church once a month.
3 = This person attends church every other week.
4 = This person attends church one time a week.
5 = This person attends church twice a week or more.

QUESTION:	ANSWER:
20. What part do you play in church activities?	

SUBSCALE: B. Active-Passive Involvement
RATING:
1 = This person completely avoids participation in worship or other religious activities.
2 = an answer judged to be between 1 and 3.
3 = This person participates when asked, but does not initiate involvement.
4 = an answer judged to be between 3 and 5.
5 = This person shows active involvement and commitment in worship and other religious activities.

QUESTION:	ANSWER:
21. Do you give money to the church or other religious organizations? What percentage of your income would you estimate you give?	

SUBSCALE: C. Commitment of Finances
RATING:
1 = This person gives no money to the church.
2 = an answer judged to be between 1 and 3.

3 = This person gives periodically to the church, but less than 10% of his/her income.

4 = an answer judged to be between 3 and 5.

5 = This person regularly gives 10% or more of his/her income to the church.

QUESTION: ANSWER:

22. Why do you attend
    church?

SUBSCALE: D. Reason for Involvement
RATING:

1 = This person views involvement in a religious community as unnecessary for expression of his/her faith.

2 = an answer judged to be between 1 and 3.

3 = This person is ambivalent about the importance of his/her involvement in a religious community.

4 = an answer judged to be between 3 and 5.

5 = This person is involved in church or group as an expression of a desire to grow in his/her faith (i.e., service, study, fellowship, worship).

4 = an answer judged to be between 3 and 5.

3 = This person is involved for both social gain and expression of his/her faith.

2 = an answer judged to be between 1 and 3.

1 = This person is involved in a church or religious group solely for emotional or status needs, rather than to grow in his/her faith.

VI. Experiencing Fellowship

QUESTION: ANSWER:

23. Tell me about your
    friendships?
    Who are they?
    Where did you meet
    them? How close
    are you to them?

SUBSCALE: A. Intimacy with Other Believers
RATING:
1 = This person is excessively dependent on other believers as a means of protecting him/herself from non-Christian influences.
2 = an answer judged to be between 1 and 3.
3 = This person seems to overly rely on relationships with Christians, and to neglect his/her relationships with non-Christians.
4 = an answer judged to be between 3 and 5.
5 = This person experiences relationships at various levels of intimacy, including interdependent, growth-oriented, intimate relationships with at least a few believers and a few non-believers (family, friends).
4 = an answer judged to be between 3 and 5.
3 = This person has very few intimate relationships with believers.
2 = an answer judged to be between 1 and 3.
1 = This person totally lacks intimate relationships with either Christians or non-Christians, perhaps feeling isolated, estranged and suspicious.

QUESTION: ANSWER:
24. What does being
      part of the family
      of God mean to you?

SUBSCALE: B. Identification as a Child of God
RATING:
1 = This person expresses a sense of exclusiveness in his/her identity with the family of God. This individual may display a self-righteous, judgmental attitude or condemn others who express their faith differently.
2 = an answer judged to be between 1 and 3.
3 = This person's identity with the family of God includes some sense of superiority over those seen to be outside the family of God.

4 = an answer judged to be between 3 and 5.
5 = This person identifies positively with the family of God, including a sense of community with the "people of God" and an attitude of humble appreciation for salvation.

QUESTION: ANSWER:
25. How do you feel about
    people from different
    cultures or races?

SUBSCALE: C. Identification with Humanity
RATING:
1 = This person displays a parochial, ethnocentric attitude an overidentification with one subculture, group or sect only, excluding all unlike self.
2 = an answer judged to be between 1 and 3.
3 = This person identifies with humanity to some degree, but shows considerable favoritism for his/her own group.
4 = an answer judged to be between 3 and 5.
5 = This person expresses an identification with all of humanity, a sense of commonality as God's creatures.

VII. Being Ethical

QUESTION: ANSWER:
26. How do you decide
    what is right or
    wrong?

SUBSCALE: A. Ethical Commitment and Flexibility
RATING:
1 = This person lacks clear commitment to meaningful ethical principles for his/her life.
2 = an answer judged to be between 1 and 3.

3 = This person has commitment to ethical principles, but the commitment is weak or ill-defined.

4 = an answer judged to be between 3 and 5.

5 = This person follows his/her ethical principles in a flexible but committed manner.

4 = an answer judged to be between 3 and 5.

3 = This person is committed to some ethical principles, but lacks some flexibility.

2 = an answer judged to be between 1 and 3.

1 = This person views his/her ethical principles as absolute law, following them in a very rigid manner.

QUESTION: ANSWER:

27. How does your
    faith influence
    your sense of what
    is right and wrong?

SUBSCALE: B. Relationship between Faith and Ethics
RATING:

1 = This person's faith is completely unrelated to his/her ethics. This person's ethics may be based primarily on a social convention or a fear of punishment.

2 = an answer judged to be between 1 and 3.

3 = This person's ethics are affected by both social convention and some less integrated aspects of his/her faith.

4 = an answer judged to be between 3 and 5.

5 = This person's religious faith strongly underlies and guides all of his/her ethics

---

QUESTION: ANSWER:

28. What personal and
    social ethical issues
    are you concerned
    about and how do you
    deal with them?

SUBSCALE: C. Emphasis on Personal and Social Ethics
RATING:
1 = This person expresses no concern about either personal or social ethics.
2 = an answer judged to be between 1 and 3.
3 = This person neglects either personal or social ethics.
4 = an answer judged to be between 3 and 5.
5 = This person shows concern for personal and social ethics. He/she acts from awareness of both and is concerned about individual responsibility and social justice.

QUESTION: ANSWER:
29. What satisfaction
    do you receive
    from your job, vocation,
    or what you do?

SUBSCALE: D. Serving Others in Work Situation
RATING:
1 = This person is very self-centered in his/her work or vocation, focusing only on his/her own status, financial or social needs.
2 = an answer judged to be between 1 and 3.
3 = This person focuses his/her motivations partially on his/her own needs and partially on the needs of others.
4 = an answer judged to be between 3 and 5.
5 = This person has a sense that he/she is serving others in his/her work or vocation, rather than just focusing on his/her own needs.

VIII. Affirming Openness in Faith

QUESTION: ANSWER:
30. How does your
    faith affect
    different aspects
    of your life?

SUBSCALE: A. Centrality of Faith
RATING:
1 = This person's faith is very compartmentalized, in that it does not seem to relate to any other aspects of life.
2 = an answer judged to be between 1 and 3.
3 = This person's faith is only moderately related to some aspects of his/her life.
4 = an answer judged to be between 3 and 5.
5 = This person's faith provides a directive for all aspects of his/her life.

QUESTION:	ANSWER:
31. How many times during the past year did you do some reading about your faith or had some discussions about faith with others.	

SUBSCALE: B. Growth in Faith
RATING:
1 = This person spent no time in the last year discussing or reading about his/her faith.
2 = an answer judged to be between 1 and 3.
3 = This person spent considerable time in the last year discussing or reading about his/her faith, but expressed no desire to grow in faith, reflecting instead motives of duty or habit.
4 = an answer judged to be between 3 and 5.
5 = This person spent significant time in the last year reading about his/her faith and/or discussing it with others, as an expression of a desire to grow in faith.

QUESTION:	ANSWER:
32. How do you respond to people who do not believe like you do?	

SUBSCALE: C. Openness to Divergent Viewpoints
RATING:

1 = This person's faith is very rigid and unable to tolerate differing ideas. This individual may reject or distort these different ideas and practices in order to maintain his/her own position.

2 = an answer judged to be between 1 and 3.

3 = This person is unable to tolerate new ideas in some areas of faith.

4 = an answer judged to be between 3 and 5.

5 = While expressing confidence in his/her own view, this person shows a tolerance of other's viewpoints and a willingness to examine and try to understand other people's beliefs.

4 = an answer judged to be between 3 and 5.

3 = This person is easily influenced by others' beliefs and frequently vacillates among them.

2 = an answer judged to be between 1 and 3.

1 = This person is unsure about his/her beliefs. His/her beliefs change completely depending upon whom he/she is with.

QUESTION: **ANSWER:**

33. Can you name some dimensions; or parts, of your faith that are important to you.

SUBSCALE: D. Differentiation of Faith
RATING:

1 = This person's faith is thoroughly undifferentiated and composed of a small number of categories or elements. Ideas are global and overgeneralized. (1 part)

2 = an answer judged to be between 1 and 3.

3 = This person's faith is composed of only a few categories or elements. These ideas include generalizations. (3 parts)

4 = an answer judged to be between 3 and 5.
5 = This person's faith is differentiated and is composed of a relatively large number of categories or elements. Ideas are multiple and specific rather than overgeneralized. (5 parts)

Religious Status Inventory[1]

Instructions

This inventory contains 160 items designed to study the way people think about their Christian faith and how it interacts with their lives. It may be taken by those who consider themselves Christians. Items will reflect what you believe, feel, and do, in connection with your faith. There are no right or wrong answers. Just answer what is true for you.

On the answer sheet provided for you please write your name and other information which has been asked for. Then begin by reading each statement and deciding whether this is true of you or not true of you. For each item indicate on the answer sheet a number representing the following answers:

```
Not true                                True
of me                                   of me
 |--------|---------|---------|--------|
 1        2         3         4        5
```

As you answer the items, please keep the following in mind:

1. Using a number 2 pencil, darken the appropriate circle on the answer sheet completely.
2. Respond to each statement as it is true for you. It is best to say what you really believe, feel, or do.

---

[1] Copyright © 1988 by David E. Massey and Mark N. Hadlock

3. Give the answer which comes to mind first. Don't spend too much time thinking about a question.
4. Statements may not reflect *all* the information you would like to give about yourself. Give the best possible response to the statement listed.
5. Respond to all statements. Do not skip any.

1. I'm always happy because God takes care of all my problems.
2. I have read many books about my faith in the past year.
3. Making a decision is as simple as praying to God and waiting for an answer.
4. I regularly attend church or a religious community.
5. Religion is just one aspect of my life.
6. I pray for help in my decisions rather than ask for specific answers.
7. I have little desire to read a religious book.
8. When someone asks me to forgive them I am able to do so.
9. Whatever problems I have I bring on myself.
10. I have been unable to find a group of Christians where I feel accepted.
11. I contribute a lot money for social causes.
12. When I've done something wrong I try to do something to correct the situation.
13. Both prayer and personal action are needed to deal with difficult problems. One without the other is insufficient.
14. Without my Christian faith I would be a much different person.
15. I change my religious beliefs frequently.
16. I usually find something else to do rather than go to church.
17. When God forgives me I feel like I'm "off the hook."
18. I would be free of problems if life treated me better.
19. There are a lot of different parts of my faith that I want to explore.
20. God can use my anger in positive ways.
21. I make most of my decisions based on the idea that I should do to others what I want them to do to me.
22. I feel a desire to worship God throughout the week.
23. Jesus Christ is the Lord of my life.
24. I am trying to help change many things that are unfair in the world.
25. When I've wronged someone it is useless to apologize to them.

26. I know that God will bring good out of all my painful situations because he loves me.
27. Being with non-Christians makes me feel uncomfortable.
28. It's important to do what other people want you to do.
29. God is more important to me than anything else in my life.
30. I feel accepted and understood when I am with other Christians.
31. I am conscious that my relationship to God affects how I relate to my family.
32. I decide if something is right or wrong by what happens to me.
33. I feel safe and secure knowing that God loves me.
34. When I sin I have a sense that God cares less about what happens to me.
35. I consider myself very active in moral issues.
36. I consistently give a large amount of my income to a church or religious organization.
37. It is difficult for me to relate to Christians who believe differently than I do.
38. When making major decisions I ask for help from my family, friends and God.
39. I trust that the future is in God's hands and that I will accept whatever he has for me.
40. I need God's help in every minor decision I make.
41. One reason I go to church is to feel important in my community.
42. Denominational differences mean little to me.
43. When I am with a group of Christians I feel at home.
44. I feel good about what I do because I know I am contributing to society.
45. I have little desire to be involved in social action.
46. Receiving God's forgiveness inspires me to worship and praise God.
47. I feel comfortable receiving God's love and forgiveness.
48. All I can do is take what comes in life.

49. When I have hurt someone I feel so guilty that I find myself avoiding them.
50. I fail to understand why things have to happen to me.
51. It bothers me that God does so little to make my life better.
52. I try to keep my religion separate from other aspects of my life.
53. I lack direction from God in how to fulfill my roles with my work and family.
54. If someone hurts me it makes it hard for me to trust them again.
55. I have a regular devotional time in order to grow in my faith.
56. Some problems and sins are so complex that it is difficult to put blame on any one thing.
57. I expect some hard times in the future but trust that God will help me through them.
58. I have difficulty handling someone getting angry at me.
59. I feel a common bond with other Christians.
60. God is an impersonal force.
61. I can do little to make my future better.
62. I'm uneasy around people from different cultures or races.
63. I am quick to ask for forgiveness when I have hurt someone.
64. I consistently go to church or a religious community twice a week or more.
65. My religious beliefs should be kept separate from what I do in my daily life.
66. I can know God merely by interacting with people.
67. I respect beliefs that are different from mine.
68. The causes of my problems include both myself and my surroundings.
69. Prayer helps me feel closer to God.
70. I am involved in my community as an expression of my faith.
71. I continue to wish the best for someone who has hurt me.
72. I volunteer quite often for church positions.
73. Prayer is useless in helping make major decisions.
74. I enjoy being around

other people of different cultures or races.

75. I think about what God would want for my life when I make any major decision.

76. I have a great deal of problem with people who feel that our culture is better than others.

77. I see Jesus mainly as the founder of Christianity.

78. I feel forgiven by God when I sin.

79. It bothers me when religious differences keep people from becoming friends.

80. I would lose interest in my job if it paid less.

81. In the midst of prayer I sometimes stop and just listen.

82. Sometimes anger allows me to be productive in my actions.

83. I rarely go to church or a religious community.

84. I stand in awe and wonder of God my creator.

85. To make Jesus relevant to my daily life seems to be taking religion too far.

86. I continue to give money to the church during times when it is hard to pay my bills.

87. As a Christian everything is wonderful and will continue to be.

88. I have close friendships with both Christians and non-Christians.

89. God punishes sin.

90. I am careful to do what is right for fear that I will be punished by God.

91. I fail to see how my religious life relates to what I do every day.

92. Often I wonder if God really forgives me.

93. When problems are difficult I recognize there is nothing I can do so I give it all to God.

94. My faith affects every aspect of my life.

95. My main reason for going to church is to make me feel better.

96. When I think of God's love I get a warm and tender feeling inside.

97. I believe that God has a purpose for me in my job or what I do.

98. I seldom take time to think about my relationship with God.

99. My decisions are always founded on my faith.

100. Pain makes me question God's role in my life.
101. I have a hard time accepting God's forgiveness because I feel unworthy to receive it.
102. It is hard to be open and honest with other Christians.
103. I feel good about how God uses me in what I do.
104. When I have wronged someone my first thought is how that person might be feeling.
105. I lack close relationships with any group of Christians.
106. I rarely give money to the church.
107. I expect to have both good times and bad times in my future.
108. People from other cultures who become Christians will need to give up much of their cultural lifestyle.
109. I try to serve God through my work.
110. I have little desire to give money to the church.
111. The church lacks a feeling of being like a family to me.
112. I rarely consider what God would think about my actions.
113. I enjoy my work because it makes me feel good about myself.
114. When someone has wronged me I give them the cold shoulder.
115. What is right or wrong is sometimes unclear.
116. I refuse to listen to someone who says things contrary to the Bible.
117. I rely solely on my own resources to make major decisions in my life.
118. People from some cultures or races are difficult to trust.
119. Suffering seems to develop and refine my faith and character.
120. I need friendships with both Christians and non-Christians to help me grow.
121. God will still love me regardless of what I do.
122. Without my faith in God I would be lacking much of my sense of what is right or wrong.
123. I live my life without need of God's assistance.
124. When I have hurt

someone I try to ask myself what I can do to make it right.

125. My faith is renewed when I attend church.

126. I seldom struggle with decisions of what is right or wrong.

127. I avoid volunteering for church positions.

128. I need to be more involved in church than just being a member.

129. If you follow the Bible you will know what is right or wrong in all situations.

130. The main reason I worship God is that I feel I should.

131. Involvement in a religious community seems unnecessary to me.

132. I avoid churches that encourage a lot of involvement.

133. I don't get angry.

134. I try to keep a balance between what I can do for myself and what God can do for me.

135. It is important for Christians to separate themselves from non-Christians.

136. It would be hard to refrain from worshiping God.

137. Both God's guidance and my capabilities are important for dealing with difficult situations.

138. It's hard for me to understand how other people get so excited about God's love.

139. My concern for others is based on my love for God.

140. Knowing God loves me gets me very excited.

141. I am comfortable with other people believing differently than I.

142. I go to church mainly to worship God and fellowship with other Christians.

143. If I've done something wrong it is better to let it go than to bring it up again and apologize for it.

144. Because God loves and forgives me it makes me want to go out of my way to help someone else.

145. I pray mainly when things are out of my control.

146. I have little need to deal with moral issues because very few affect me.

147. I like to just sit and enjoy a church service.

I dislike being asked to participate in it.

148. My religious beliefs are complex.
149. I feel an absence of God's love in my life.
150. I go to church because I want to grow as a Christian.
151. I feel guilty when I fail to pray.
152. Talking to people from different cultures helps me to have a broader view of life.
153. Some people would say that my faith is too simple.
154. I am very active in church activities.
155. To know that God loves me is the only thing I need to know about my faith.
156. God is disappointed with me when I get angry.
157. I have discussed my faith with others on many occasions within the past year.
158. I live my daily life without thinking about my religious beliefs.
159. Discussing my faith with others seems unnecessary.
160. I try to keep an open mind about other beliefs and am willing to change my beliefs if necessary.

The Psychology of Religion for Ministry

Answer Sheet

Name _____

Please fill in information as directed in the space below.

1. 1 2 3 4 5	2. 1 2 3 4 5	3. 1 2 3 4 5
4. 1 2 3 4 5	5. 1 2 3 4 5	6. 1 2 3 4 5
7. 1 2 3 4 5	8. 1 2 3 4 5	9. 1 2 3 4 5
10. 1 2 3 4 5	11. 1 2 3 4 5	12. 1 2 3 4 5
13. 1 2 3 4 5	14. 1 2 3 4 5	15. 1 2 3 4 5
16. 1 2 3 4 5	17. 1 2 3 4 5	18. 1 2 3 4 5
19. 1 2 3 4 5	20. 1 2 3 4 5	21. 1 2 3 4 5
22. 1 2 3 4 5	23. 1 2 3 4 5	24. 1 2 3 4 5
25. 1 2 3 4 5	26. 1 2 3 4 5	27. 1 2 3 4 5
28. 1 2 3 4 5	29. 1 2 3 4 5	30. 1 2 3 4 5
31. 1 2 3 4 5	32. 1 2 3 4 5	33. 1 2 3 4 5
34. 1 2 3 4 5	35. 1 2 3 4 5	36. 1 2 3 4 5
37. 1 2 3 4 5	38. 1 2 3 4 5	39. 1 2 3 4 5
40. 1 2 3 4 5	41. 1 2 3 4 5	42. 1 2 3 4 5
43. 1 2 3 4 5	44. 1 2 3 4 5	45. 1 2 3 4 5
46. 1 2 3 4 5	47. 1 2 3 4 5	48. 1 2 3 4 5
49. 1 2 3 4 5	50. 1 2 3 4 5	51. 1 2 3 4 5
52. 1 2 3 4 5	53. 1 2 3 4 5	54. 1 2 3 4 5
55. 1 2 3 4 5	56. 1 2 3 4 5	57. 1 2 3 4 5
58. 1 2 3 4 5	59. 1 2 3 4 5	60. 1 2 3 4 5
61. 1 2 3 4 5	62. 1 2 3 4 5	63. 1 2 3 4 5
64. 1 2 3 4 5	65. 1 2 3 4 5	66. 1 2 3 4 5
67. 1 2 3 4 5	68. 1 2 3 4 5	69. 1 2 3 4 5
70. 1 2 3 4 5	71. 1 2 3 4 5	72. 1 2 3 4 5
73. 1 2 3 4 5	74. 1 2 3 4 5	75. 1 2 3 4 5
76. 1 2 3 4 5	77. 1 2 3 4 5	78. 1 2 3 4 5
79. 1 2 3 4 5	80. 1 2 3 4 5	81. 1 2 3 4 5
82. 1 2 3 4 5	83. 1 2 3 4 5	84. 1 2 3 4 5
85. 1 2 3 4 5	86. 1 2 3 4 5	87. 1 2 3 4 5
88. 1 2 3 4 5	89. 1 2 3 4 5	90. 1 2 3 4 5
91. 1 2 3 4 5	92. 1 2 3 4 5	93. 1 2 3 4 5
94. 1 2 3 4 5	95. 1 2 3 4 5	96. 1 2 3 4 5

97. 1 2 3 4 5   98. 1 2 3 4 5   99. 1 2 3 4 5
100. 1 2 3 4 5   101. 1 2 3 4 5   102. 1 2 3 4 5
103. 1 2 3 4 5   104. 1 2 3 4 5   105. 1 2 3 4 5
106. 1 2 3 4 5   107. 1 2 3 4 5   108. 1 2 3 4 5
109. 1 2 3 4 5   110. 1 2 3 4 5   111. 1 2 3 4 5
112. 1 2 3 4 5   113. 1 2 3 4 5   114. 1 2 3 4 5
115. 1 2 3 4 5   116. 1 2 3 4 5   117. 1 2 3 4 5
118. 1 2 3 4 5   119. 1 2 3 4 5   120. 1 2 3 4 5
121. 1 2 3 4 5   122. 1 2 3 4 5   123. 1 2 3 4 5
124. 1 2 3 4 5   125. 1 2 3 4 5   126. 1 2 3 4 5
127. 1 2 3 4 5   128. 1 2 3 4 5   129. 1 2 3 4 5
130. 1 2 3 4 5   131. 1 2 3 4 5   132. 1 2 3 4 5
133. 1 2 3 4 5   134. 1 2 3 4 5   135. 1 2 3 4 5
136. 1 2 3 4 5   137. 1 2 3 4 5   138. 1 2 3 4 5
139. 1 2 3 4 5   140. 1 2 3 4 5   141. 1 2 3 4 5
142. 1 2 3 4 5   143. 1 2 3 4 5   144. 1 2 3 4 5
145. 1 2 3 4 5   146. 1 2 3 4 5   147. 1 2 3 4 5
148. 1 2 3 4 5   149. 1 2 3 4 5   150. 1 2 3 4 5
151. 1 2 3 4 5   152. 1 2 3 4 5   153. 1 2 3 4 5
154. 1 2 3 4 5   155. 1 2 3 4 5   156. 1 2 3 4 5
157. 1 2 3 4 5   158. 1 2 3 4 5   159. 1 2 3 4 5
160. 1 2 3 4 5

Scoring the Religious Status Inventory

There are two ways to score the **Religious Status Inventory** (RSI). One way is by using the *Eight Dimensions* on the basis of which the RSI was originally constructed. The other way is by using the *Seven Factors* found in a factor analysis done in 1993 by Dr. Cynthia Jackson. These two alternatives are described below.

When the phrase "**Reverse Score**" is used, it means that, when you add the answers to "Reverse Score" items to the score for that Dimension or Factor, you should change all "5s" to "1s," all "2s" to "4s," and leave all "3s" as they are. This will make sense with an example:

Item 7 is "I have little desire to read a religious book." (The person taking the RSI answers along a 5-point scale where "5" equals "True of Me" and "1" equals "Not True of Me.")

Item 7 is a "Reverse Score" item on *Dimension 7*—Affirming Openness in Faith and on *Factor 1*—Religious Omissions. Since all scores on *Dimensions* and on *Factors* are additive (in the sense that you add up scores on the items to get a score for that *Dimension* or *Factor*), the "higher" the score, the more that *Dimension* or *Factor* characterizes them. Thus, it can be seen that if a participant checked "1" on this item, it should be weighted as a "5" in adding to the person being more Open in their Faith (*Dimension 7*) as well as adding to the number of things they do that should NOT do (*Factor 1*—Religious Omissions). Note that *Dimension 7* is positive; higher scores contribute to greater religious maturity while *Factor 1* is negative; higher scores contribute to less religious maturity.

Hopefully, this explanation clarified for you why some items are reverse scored.

Scoring for Dimensions of the RSI

Dimension 1 **AWARENESS OF GOD**
Items: 13 22 23 29 69 81   84 134 136 137
(Reverse Score) 40 60 66 77 85 93 123 130 145 151

Dimension 2 **ACCEPTANCE OF GOD'S GRACE AND STEADFAST LOVE**
Items: 26 33 46 47 78 96 119 121 140 144
(Reverse Score) 1 17 34 50 89 92 100 101 138 149

Dimension 3 **KNOWING GOD'S LEADERSHIP AND DIRECTION**
Item: 6 31 38 39 57 70 75 103 107 109
(Reverse Score) 3 48 51 53 61 65 73   87   91 117

Dimension 4 **BEING ETHICAL**
Item: 11 21 24 35 44   97   99 115 122 139
(Reverse Score) 28 32 45 80 90 112 113 126 129 146

Dimension 5 **BEING REPENTANT AND RESPONSIBLE**
Item: 8 12 20 56 63 68   71   82 104 124
(Reverse Score) 9 18 25 49 54 58 114 133 143 156

Dimension 6 **INVOLVEMENT IN ORGANIZED RELIGION**
Item: 4 36 64 72   86 125 128 142 150 154
(Reverse Score) 16 41 83 95 106 110 127 131 132 147

Dimension 7 **EXPERIENCING FELLOWSHIP**
Item: 30 42 43 59 74 76 79 88 120 152
(Reverse Score) 10 27 37 62 102 105 108 111 118 135

Dimension 8 **AFFIRMING OPENNESS IN FAITH**
Item: 2 14 19 55 67   94 141 148 157 160
(Reverse Score) 5   7 15 52 98 116 153 155 158 159

The range for each **DIMENSION** is 20 to 100. **A Total Score** can be obtained by adding up all *Dimensions*. The range for the Total Score is 160 to 800.

Scoring for Factors on the RSI

Factor 1 **RELIGIOUS OMISSIONS**—66 Items
Range: 66–330

Items: 89   113   151
(Reverse Score)   7   10   15   16   18   25   27   28   32   34
                  37   41   45   48   50   51   52   53   60   61
                  62   65   66   73   77   80   83   85   87   90
                  91   92   95   98 100 102 105 106 108 110
                 111 112 114 116 117 118 123 126 127 130
                 131 132 133 135 138 143 145 146 147 149
                 155 158 159

Factor 2   **WORSHIP AND COMMITMENT**—43 Items
          Range: 43–215
Items: 4   8   12   13   14   22   23   26   29   30
          31   33   38   39   43   46   47   57   59   69
          75   78   81   84   94   96   97 103 107 109
         119 121 122 125 128 136 137 139 140 142
         144 150 157

Factor 3   **OPENNESS AND COMPLEXITY**—9 Items
          Range: 9–45
Items: 19   20   56   68   82   115   120   148   160

Factor 4   **INVOLVEMENT IN ORGANIZED RELIGION**—
          11 Items   Range: 11–55
Items: 2   11   35   36   55   64   70   72   86   99   154

Factor 5   **SIMPLE TRUST**—7 Items   Range: 7–35
Items: 1   3   17   40   93   129   156

Factor 6   **AVOIDANCE**—3 Items   Range: 3–15
Items: 49   54   101

Factor 7   **FELLOWSHIP**—13 Items   Range: 13–65
Items: 21   24   44   63   67   71   74   79   88   104   124
         141   152

A **Total Factor Score** can be obtained by adding up all the
Factor scores. The possible range is 152–760.

Means, Standard Deviations, Ranges for the Religious Status Inventory—451 Students, Colleges and Seminaries, USA

RSI scored on the basis of the 8 Original Dimensions

	Mean	Standard Deviation	Range
Awareness of God	71.96	9.52	45–95
Acceptance of God's Leadership and Direction	72.95	9.61	47–94
Being Repentant and Responsible	72.21	6.27	53–90
Knowing God's Leadership	77.87	11.21	43–98
Involvement in Organized Religion	69.06	14.57	32–98
Experiencing Fellowship	76.94	7.88	54–98
Being Ethical	70.11	6.97	50–86
Affirming Openness in Faith	72.58	9.23	43–95
TOTAL	583.69	60.72	417–726

RSI scored on the basis of Jackson's (1993) Factor Analysis

	Mean	Standard Deviation	Range
Religious Omissions	250.57	29.74	129–312
Worship and Commitment	165.14	30.93	56–212
Involvement in Organized Religion	31.82	8.13	12–50
Simple Trust	19.17	5.14	7–31
Avoidance	9.08	2.11	3–15
Fellowship	49.72	5.30	31–63
TOTAL	557.82	64.37	361–677

Adult Life Event Checklist[1]

Instructions: Below are listed a number of events that may have occurred at some time in your life. Please check the appropriate blanks if the event occurred during any of the time periods indicated.

Life Events	Within Past Year	1–5 Years Ago	Over 5 Years Ago
1. Death of spouse	____	____	____
2. Institutionalization (for example: nursing home, psychiatric hospital, prison)	____	____	____
3. Death of a close family member	____	____	____
4. Major personal injury (for example: auto accident or fall which is still a problem)	____	____	____
5. Major personal illness which is still a problem	____	____	____
6. Getting a divorce	____	____	____
7. Being fired from work	____	____	____
8. Major personal injury which is no longer a problem	____	____	____
9. Major personal illness which is no longer a problem	____	____	____
10. Major change in financial state	____	____	____
11. Retirement	____	____	____

---

[1]Bruce E. Atkinson, *Religious Maturity and Psychological Distress among Older Christian Women* (Unpublished Doctoral Dissertation, Fuller Theological Seminary, Pasadena, CA 1986).

12. Marital separation . . . . ＿＿＿ ＿＿＿ ＿＿＿
13. Being physically or sexually
    abused. . . . . ＿＿＿ ＿＿＿ ＿＿＿
14. Getting married . . . . ＿＿＿ ＿＿＿ ＿＿＿
15. Death of a close friend . . . . ＿＿＿ ＿＿＿ ＿＿＿
16. Major change to a family member or relative (including
    health, finances, relationships). ＿＿＿ ＿＿＿ ＿＿＿
17. Major change in gratifying
    activities . . . . ＿＿＿ ＿＿＿ ＿＿＿
18. Major change in sexual
    behavior . . . . ＿＿＿ ＿＿＿ ＿＿＿
19. Major change in work
    responsibilities . . . . ＿＿＿ ＿＿＿ ＿＿＿
20. Change in residence . . . . ＿＿＿ ＿＿＿ ＿＿＿
21. Changing to a different line
    of work . . . . ＿＿＿ ＿＿＿ ＿＿＿
22. Pregnancy . . . . ＿＿＿ ＿＿＿ ＿＿＿
23. Spouse starting or stopping
    work. . . . . ＿＿＿ ＿＿＿ ＿＿＿
24. Major change in living conditions or
    environment . . . . ＿＿＿ ＿＿＿ ＿＿＿
25. Marital reconciliation . . . . ＿＿＿ ＿＿＿ ＿＿＿
26. Major business readjustment (bankruptcy, relocation,
    merger). . . . . ＿＿＿ ＿＿＿ ＿＿＿
27. Major change in social
    activities . . . . ＿＿＿ ＿＿＿ ＿＿＿
28. Major increase in family
    arguments . . . . ＿＿＿ ＿＿＿ ＿＿＿
29. Losing driver's license . . . . ＿＿＿ ＿＿＿ ＿＿＿
30. Major change in number of persons living
    in the home . . . . ＿＿＿ ＿＿＿ ＿＿＿
31. Reaching 65 years of age . . . . . . ＿＿＿ ＿＿＿ ＿＿＿
32. Reaching 70 years of age . . . . . . ＿＿＿ ＿＿＿ ＿＿＿
33. Major in-law troubles . . . . ＿＿＿ ＿＿＿ ＿＿＿
34. Major change in working hours
    or conditions . . . . ＿＿＿ ＿＿＿ ＿＿＿
35. Major troubles with the boss. . . . ＿＿＿ ＿＿＿ ＿＿＿

36. Holidays, anniversaries spent
    alone .... _____   _____   _____
37. Outstanding personal
    achievement .... _____   _____   _____
38. Major revision of personal
    habits....................... _____   _____   _____

Please check if any of these events occurred during childhood
or adolescence:

39. Unwed pregnancy .... _____
40. Divorce of parents............................ _____
41. Marital separation of parents .... _____
42. Having a visible physical deformity .... _____
43. Becoming involved with alcohol or drugs .... _____
44. Jail sentence of a parent....................... _____
45. Discovery of being adopted .... _____
46. Major change in acceptance by childhood peers. _____
47. Marriage of parent to a step-parent .... _____
48. Pregnancy in an unwed teenage sister .... _____
49. Failure of a grade in school.................... _____
50. Frequently changing schools .... _____

                                    Total: _____

ALEC Scoring Key (in Life Change Units)

Life Events	Full Score	.7	.3
1. Death of spouse	125	88	38
2. Institutionalization................	82	57	25
3. Death of a close family member....	67	47	20
4. Personal injury, still problem	67	47	20
5. Personal illness, still problem	67	47	20
6. Getting a divorce	64	45	19
7. Being fired from work.............	64	45	19
8. Personal injury, not a problem now	57	40	17
9. Personal illness, not a problem now	57	40	17

10.	Major change in financial state	56	39	17
11.	Retirement	55	39	17
12.	Marital separation	54	38	16
13.	Being physically or sexually abused	54	38	16
14.	Getting married	50	35	15
15.	Death of a close friend	50	35	15
16.	Change to a family member	47	33	14
17.	Change in gratifying activities	46	32	14
18.	Major change in sexual behavior	45	31	13
19.	Change in work responsibilities	43	30	13
20.	Change in residence	43	30	13
21.	Changing to different line of work	41	29	12
22.	Pregnancy	40	28	12
23.	Spouse starting or stopping work	40	28	12
24.	Change in living conditions	40	28	12
25.	Marital reconciliation	39	27	12
26.	Major business readjustment	39	27	12
27.	Major change in social activities	38	27	11
28.	Major increase in family arguments	35	25	11
29.	Losing driver's license	34	24	10
30.	Change in number of persons in home	33	23	10
31.	Reaching 65 years of age	32	22	10
32.	Reaching 70 years of age	31	22	9
33.	Major in-law troubles	29	20	9
34.	Change in working conditions	28	20	8
35.	Major troubles with the boss	28	20	8
36.	Holidays, anniversaries spent alone	28	20	8
37.	Outstanding personal achievement	28	20	8
38.	Major revision of personal habits	24	17	7

Childhood or adolescence:		.1
39.	Unwed pregnancy	10
40.	Divorce of parents	9
41.	Marital separation of parents	9
42.	Having a visible physical deformity	8
43.	Becoming involved with alcohol or drugs	8
44.	Jail sentence of a parent	8

45. Discovery of being adopted...................... 7
46. Major change in acceptance by childhood peers .. 6
47. Marriage of parent to a step-parent.............. 6
48. Pregnancy in an unwed teenage sister 6
49. Failure of a grade in school 6
50. Frequently changing schools.................... 5

Appendix VI

=======================

Ministerial Effectiveness Inventory[1]

INSTRUCTIONS: Read each of the following statements and rate the above minister, based on your impression, as to how frequently each statement is characteristic of him/her. Use your best judgment when personal experience is unavailable. Please circle your response for each statement and without pondering, give the initial rating that comes to mind. Answer for every statement. Response ratings range from "Never" to "Always."

Minister Evaluated

How characteristic of the minister is this?

NEVER   ALWAYS

1) This minister questions whether he/she should be in ministry. 1 2 3 4 5 6

2) This minister promotes a sense of mutuality in the entire worshiping community. 1 2 3 4 5 6

---

[1] Laura F. Majovski, *Predicting Ministerial Effectiveness on the Basis of Psychological Evaluations* (Unpublished Doctoral Dissertation, Fuller Theological Seminary, Pasadena, CA, 1981).

	Minister Evaluated

<u>Remember:</u>   For each statement answer this question: How characteristic of the minister is this?

How characteristic of the minister is this?

	NEVER				ALWAYS

3) This minister acts in ethical or professional ways that violate principles to protect self.

    1   2   3   4   5   6

4) This minister uses an administrative style that implies shared leadership and that builds persons into a cooperative community.

    1   2   3   4   5   6

5) This minister uses a style of leadership that is flexible and responsible.

    1   2   3   4   5   6

6) This minister acts in ways that suggest that his/her family life is a high priority.

    1   2   3   4   5   6

7) This minister reflects coldness and immaturity in his/her actions.

    1   2   3   4   5   6

8) This minister has an approach to ministry that reflects a deep personal faith commitment.

    1   2   3   4   5   6

9) This minister demonstrates a style of life-long learning, through continued education, research, and study.   1   2   3   4   5   6

10) This minister has a knowledge of general information which he/she uses to make decisions.   1   2   3   4   5   6

11) This minister's approach to ministry emphasizes evangelistic and mission goals.   1   2   3   4   5   6

12) This minister expresses respect and sympathy in his/her actions.   1   2   3   4   5   6

13) This minister uses a facilitative and trusting style of leadership.   1   2   3   4   5   6

14) This minister preaches with competence and sensitivity.   1   2   3   4   5   6

15) This minister has basic knowledge of the Methodist denominational workings.   1   2   3   4   5   6

16) This minister recognizes his/her own commonality with spiritual problems of the congregation.   1   2   3   4   5   6

17) This minister is readily available to counsel persons experiencing stress.   1   2   3   4   5   6

_____

Minister Evaluated

Remember: For each statement
answer this ques-   How characteristic of the
tion: How charac-   minister is this?
teristic of the minis-
ter is this?

NEVER   ALWAYS

18) This minister leads worship   1   2   3   4   5   6
in aesthetically sensitive
ways.

19) This minister behaves re-   1   2   3   4   5   6
sponsibly towards persons
as well as tasks.

20) This minister uses a leader-   1   2   3   4   5   6
ship style that properly uti-
lizes conflict.

21) This minister assumes a   1   2   3   4   5   6
nondefensive professional
role in his/her actions.

22) This minister's lifestyle in-   1   2   3   4   5   6
volves occasional excessive
use of alcohol and/or smok-
ing.

23) This minister uses psycho-   1   2   3   4   5   6
logically informed counsel-
ing skills.

24) This minister reveals a hu-   1   2   3   4   5   6
man image of ministry.

25) This minister shows indications of professional immaturity in ministry.　　1　2　3　4　5　6

26) This minister assumes a patient, hopeful role in dealing with people.　　1　2　3　4　5　6

27) This minister has a self-serving ministry characterized by irresponsibility.　　1　2　3　4　5　6

28) This minister shows evidence of personal growth.　　1　2　3　4　5　6

29) This minister frightens people off with his/her dominating, superior attitude.　　1　2　3　4　5　6

30) This minister gains financial support for the church while remaining sensitive to persons.　　1　2　3　4　5　6

31) This minister has a personal family style which is consistent with his/her ministry.　　1　2　3　4　5　6

32) This minister speaks about theological issues in understandable language.　　1　2　3　4　5　6

33) This minister applies theological understanding to a conscious examination of his/her own life.　　1　2　3　4　5　6

	Minister Evaluated

<u>Remember:</u> For each statement answer this question: How characteristic of the minister is this?

How characteristic of the minister is this?

	NEVER				ALWAYS	

34) This minister's attitude is sexist, pessimistic and condemning.   1   2   3   4   5   6

35) This minister has an approach to ministry that is centered in strong biblical affirmation.   1   2   3   4   5   6

36) This minister has a positive style of ministry.   1   2   3   4   5   6

37) This minister entertains ambitions inconsistent with ministerial calling.   1   2   3   4   5   6

38) This minister evidences theological resources in counseling.   1   2   3   4   5   6

39) This minister's style of leadership is efficient.   1   2   3   4   5   6

40) This minister encourages relationships of trust between himself/herself and the congregation.   1   2   3   4   5   6

41) This minister seems to need constant reassurance.　1　2　3　4　5　6

42) This minister counsels with empathic understanding and involvement.　1　2　3　4　5　6

43) This minister shows indications of the pursuit of personal advantage in ministry.　1　2　3　4　5　6

44) This minister indicates professional preparation in pastoral care.　1　2　3　4　5　6

45) This minister uses a style of ministry that is open and flexible.　1　2　3　4　5　6

46) This minister uses theological understanding that is built on careful thought and reflection.　1　2　3　4　5　6

47) This minister seems far more concerned with self than others.　1　2　3　4　5　6

48) This minister shows honesty with self and congregation.　1　2　3　4　5　6

49) This minister is fearful of participation in programs of social change.　1　2　3　4　5　6

50) This minister is sensitive to matters of ministerial protocol.　1　2　3　4　5　6

Remember: For each statement
answer this ques-
tion: How charac-
teristic of the minis-
ter is this?

		Minister Evaluated			

How characteristic of the
minister is this?

	NEVER				ALWAYS	
51) This minister encourages, recruits, and gives meaningful tasks to persons in the congregation.	1	2	3	4	5	6
52) This minister acts with openness, innovation, and eagerness to share in the life of the community as a private citizen.	1	2	3	4	5	6
53) This minister indicates that he/she knows the members well.	1	2	3	4	5	6
54) This minister rejects priestly definitions of ministry.	1	2	3	4	5	6
55) This minister's attitude is compulsive and demeaning.	1	2	3	4	5	6
56) This minister has a self-serving ministry characterized by undisciplined living.	1	2	3	4	5	6
57) This minister understands the value of openness with other Methodist professionals.	1	2	3	4	5	6

58) This minister's lifestyle in- 1   2   3   4   5   6
volves illicit sexual activity
and/or gambling.

59) This minister enables the 1   2   3   4   5   6
congregation to experience
opportunities for personal
grcwth and spiritual enrich-
ment.

*How long have you known this minister? _____

****Thank you for your completion of this questionnaire.****

*Omitted on Pastor Rating Form.

Scoring the Ministerial Effectiveness Inventory

All items are scored at face value except the following:
   1, 3, 7, 22, 25, 27, 29, 34, 37, 41, 43, 47, 49, 54, 55, 56, 58.

These items are scored in the opposite direction, i.e., when assigned a rating of 4, for the purposes of scoring the completed questionnaire, the item would be counted as a 2.

These items are scored in the opposite direction due to the negative content of the item. Total possible score is 354.